Published by Walter T. Kelley Co., Inc.
P.O. Box 240, Clarkson, KY 42726

First Edition

Printed in the U.S.A. by Great River Printing Company
Hamilton, Illinois

ISBN 0-9713523-0-5

Beekeeping Principles

A Manual for the Beginner
A Guide for the Gardener

By:

James E. Tew, Ph.D.

The Ohio State University
Wooster, OH 44691

Published by:

The Walter T. Kelley Company
3107 Elizabethtown Road
Clarkson, Kentucky 42726-0240

November, 2000

Acknowledgements

To my wife Vallie, and my parents, James and Gerry Tew, for paying for my education; to Sarah Manion at the W. T. Kelley Company for her patience; to Sherry Ferrell and Dave Heilman, my coworkers at The Ohio State University; to Uncle Auby, who got me my first hive; and to all the beekeepers, both past and present, who helped make me one, too. Thanks.

Foreword

While making significant changes during the past twenty years, beekeeping has essentially stayed the same. How can that be? Bees still swarm in the spring. Honey is still produced during the early summer and must be extracted. Bee related pollination tasks are still critical to plant propagation and are still appreciated by growers and gardeners. These characteristics have not changed.

So what has changed? We have to control predacious mites and tame rogue strains of bees. We have had to learn to use chemicals responsibly within the hive, and we have had to learn to co-exist with concerned neighbors who fear stings and occasionally threaten legal action. We have new types of equipment to incorporate and new procedures to learn. While many aspects of beekeeping are the same as they have been for hundreds of years, other aspects are now radically different.

Almost any good bee book—of any age—still contains some useful information. While such a book could answer all the old questions, it probably could not answer any of the new questions. As best I could, I have kept the old, established information, but have included new information and procedures that will help beekeepers keep bees in modern ways.

Beekeeping, as always, is still enjoyable and rewarding—a craft that many of us will pursue for a lifetime. That characteristic has not changed. Good luck in your beekeeping endeavor.

James E. Tew
The Ohio State University

Table of Contents

TABLE OF FIGURES 8

Chapter   *Page*

1. IS BEEKEEPING FOR YOU?
    AN OVERVIEW OF BEES AND BEEKEEPERS 13

2. THE BEEKEEPER'S EQUIPMENT 16
    Bee Hive Equipment 16
    Frame Assembly and Foundation Installation .27
    The Beekeeper's Protective Equipment 31
    The Smoker and Its Use 32
    The Hive Tool 33

3. BUYING EXISTING COLONIES OF HONEY BEES 35

4. STARTING HIVES FROM PACKAGE BEES 37

5. HIVING SWARMS 41
    Bee Beards—Unique Swarms Hanging In Unique Places 44

6. THE ANNUAL HIVE MANAGEMENT CYCLE—AN OVERVIEW . .46
    Major Annual Hive Management Tasks 47
    Minor Annual Hive Management Tasks 47

7. SPRING & SUMMER MANAGEMENT OF BEE COLONIES 48
    Early Spring 48
    Later Spring Management 49
    Summer Management 49

8. THE FALL & WINTER SEASON 51
    The Fall Season 51
    Combining Colonies 52
    The Winter Season 53
    Key Points for Over-Wintering Honey Bee Colonies 57
    The Winter-Killed Colony 58

9. SUPPLEMENTAL SUGAR FEEDING—HELPING A HUNGRY COLONY. . .60
    Open Feeding 61
    External Feeders 62
    Internal Feeders 62
    Comb Fillers 64
    Dry Feed 64
    Types of Sugar to Feed Bees 65
    Feeding Bees in Cool Weather 65

10.   LOCATIONS OF BEE YARDS 66
     Characteristics That Locations Must Have 66

11.   MOVING BEE COLONIES 68
     Reasons for Moving Bee Colonies 68
     A Short Move with a Few Colonies 68
     Equipment for a Commercial Move 72
     Potential Problems 72

12.   ROBBING BEHAVIOR OF HONEY BEES 74
     What is Robbing Behavior? 74
     How to Control Robbing....................................75
     Robber Bee Behavior 76
     Progressive Robbing 76

13.   BEES IN THE GARDEN 77

14.   TRANSFERRING A BEE COLONY FROM A BUILDING OR A TREE ...83
     Two Procedures for Removing Bees from Natural Nest Sites 84
     Management of the Transferred Colony 86

15.   RECORD KEEPING IN THE APIARY 87

16.   THE HONEY BEES' NEST 89

17.   THE HONEY BEE EGG 100

18.   HONEY BEE STINGING BEHAVIOR 105
     Suggestions for Avoiding a Bee Sting 106

19.   HONEY BEE ANATOMY 108
     The Adult Bee...108
     Three Body Segments 108
          The Head...108
          Thorax...109
          The Abdomen 112
     Honey Bee Anatomy Overview 112

20.   WATER NEEDS IN THE HIVE 113

21.   THE QUEEN—HER BIOLOGY, PRODUCTION & MANAGEMENT ..116
     The Modified Doolittle System of Queen Production 123

22.   LAYING WORKERS AND FALSE QUEENS 125

Laying Workers 125
False Queens 125

23. HONEY—ITS PRODUCTION, PROCESSING & PACKING 127
The Composition and Characteristics of Honey 127
Cooking With Honey 129
Honey Production 131
Spring Management for the Honey Crop 132
Removing the Honey Crop 134
Extracting and Processing the Honey Crop 136
Producing Comb Honey 139
Section Comb Honey Equipment 140
Eating Comb Honey 140
Creamed Honey Production 141
Marketing the Honey Crop 142
Selling Honey Locally 142

24. THE TWO-QUEEN SYSTEM FOR MAXIMUM
HONEY PRODUCTION 145
Advantages 147
Disadvantages 147

25. NECTAR AND POLLEN SOURCES FOR HONEY BEES 148
Plants useful to bees as food sources 149

26. POLLEN AND POLLINATION 150
Recipes for Pollen Supplement Mixes 157
Soybean Flour Dry Mix 157
Brewer's Yeast Mix (Moist Mix) 157

27. RECOGNIZING AND TREATING THE BEE HIVE FOR
COMMON DISEASES AND PESTS 159
Bacterial and Other Pathogenic Diseases 160
American Foulbrood 160
European Foulbrood 162
Nosema Disease 163
Other Commonly Occurring Diseases 164
Mite Pests of Honey Bees 164
Varroa Mites 164
Tracheal Mites 167
Insect Pests of Honey Bees 168
The Small Hive Beetle 168
Ants 170
Wax Moths 171

Chapter   *Page*

Animal Pests in the Bee Hive 172
Africanized Honey Bees in the US 174
Honey Bee Disease and Pest Identification 176

28. HONEY BEES AND PESTICIDES 177

29. BEESWAX—PRODUCTION AND PROCESSING 180
Processing Beeswax 181
Beeswax Candles 182

30. PROPOLIS—THE HIVE'S CAULKING COMPOUND 184

31. STARTING AND MAINTAINING A SMALL
OBSERVATION HIVE 186

32. MEAD—THE HONEY WINE OF THE WORLD 190

33. A SYNOPSIS OF BEEKEEPING'S HISTORY 193

34. SPECIALIZED PIECES OF BEEKEEPING EQUIPMENT 196
A Vacuum Device for Managing Bees 196
Slatted Rack 199
Drip Board 200

EPILOGUE 202

Appendix   *Page*

1. POLLEN AND NECTAR SOURCES 203
Some Major and Minor Sources of Nectar and Pollen Plants 203

2. BEESWAX CHARACTERISTICS AND USES 222
Technical Characteristics 222
Production Calculations (Estimations) 222
Processing Precautions 222
Uses for Beeswax 223

3. TREATMENT SCHEDULE 224
Generalized Treatment Schedule for Honey Bee Diseases and Pests ... 224

BIBLIOGRAPHY AND ADVANCED READINGS 225
GLOSSARY 226
INDEX 240

Table of Figures

Figure   *Page*

1. Honey bee forager on holly. 13
2. Two beekeepers working a hive. 14
3. Beekeepers learning to work a hive (circa 1920). 15
4. Bee space measurements. 16
5. Standard beehive with two hive bodies and a telescoping outer cover. ..17
6. Parts of the standard hive. 18
7. A "reversible bottom board" with the 3/4" side up and the 3/8" side down. ..19
8. An entrance reducer. 19
9. Various types of queen excluders. 20
10. A Porter Bee Escape in the handhold of an inner cover. 21
11. The inner cover with the deep side up. 22
12. A nice brood frame from a branded hive body. 23
13. Assemble hive body with the handholds to the outside............24
14. Attaching rails to the bottom board. 24
15. Box joints in the hive body. 25
16. A hive with both painted and paraffin-dipped hive bodies. 26
17. A colorful Australian beehive. 26
18. End bar attachment showing beveled upper edges. 27
19. Solid, grooved, split and two-piece bottom bars..................28
20. The correct position of the end bar nail near the beekeeper's thumb. 28
21. A selection of plastic frames. 29
22. An electric wire embedding setup. The wire embedder is lying in front of the stand. 30
23. Two fully protected beekeepers working a populous hive............31
24. A beekeeper smoking a hive. 32
25. The common, indispensable hive tool. 33
26. Good colonies for purchasing. 36
27. Packages of bees ready for shipment from a southern producer. 37
28. Shaking bees from a package...............................39
29. Bees from a recently released package. 40
30. A large, prime swarm in the apple orchard. 42
31. A bee beard team. 44
32. Spring and winter bee hives at The Ohio State University Honey Bee Laboratory. 46
33. An extremely hot hive. 50
34. Using a sheet of newspaper to combine two colonies. The edges of the paper can be seen hanging out. 51
35. A wintering honey bee cluster. 52
36. An acceptable amount of frost in the wintering hive. Some frost is not harmful, but not too much. 55
37. A hive with a wooden entrance-reducing cleat. 56

38. A winter-killed colony. 58
39. Open feeding peppermint-scented sugar syrup from a 55-gallon drum. . .61
40. A single story hive with a Boardman feeder in use. 62
41. An assortment of various hive feeders (A bucket feeder, two top
     feeders, a division board feeder, and a Boardman feeder.). 63
42. A gasoline-powered comb filler. 64
43. A good location for a bee yard. 66
44. Correct angle for inserting staples when securing a hive
     for transportation. 69
45. A nylon-ratchet-strapped hive ready for a move. 69
46. Vertical battens nailed to a hive to secure it for transportation. 70
47. A commercially manufactured entrance closing device. 71
48. A colony with a top and front screen in preparation for moving. 71
49. A commercial load of beehives. Hives are on the front and supers are
     on the back. 72
50. Bees robbing supers. 74
51. A collapsible robbing cage with an access door. 76
52. An aerial view of part of The Ohio State University bee plant garden
     (Wooster, Ohio). 77
53. A nesting box for native bee pollinators. 78
54. A prototype garden hive with a side viewing door. 80
55. A woven skep. Sizes and shapes vary. 81
56. A wild bee colony in the wall of a house. 83
57. Diagram of a screen cone trapping bees out and directing them to a
     new hive. 84
58. Beekeepers removing bees from the wall of a house. 85
59. The brick's position reminds the beekeeper of some hive need.
     In this case, the queen is not released. 87
60. A colony nesting in the open. 89
61. View of a cell base showing thirds of other three cell bases on
     the opposite side of the comb. 90
62. A comparison of honey bee cells with other common shapes.
     Hexagonal shapes are efficient in both space and building materials. . . .91
63. A bee foraging for clover nectar. 91
64. The amount of honey required to produce the wax cake. 92
65. Large pieces of burr comb. 93
66. Orienting bees fanning air over their Nasonov glands. 94
67. Dotted lines showing the dance angle. 95
68. The same dance angle on the comb. 95
69. The three kinds of bees in the hive 96
70. Queen being cared for by workers. 97
71. Worker honey bees. 97
72. Food sharing between two worker bees. This behavior distributes
     pheromones evenly throughout the colony. 98
73. A drone honey bee beside a worker. 98
74. Development times for individual stages of the worker. 99

75. The honey bee egg. 100
76. Eggs in comb. 101
77. Laying worker eggs. 103
78. A stinger being scraped off. 105
79. Major external parts of the honey bee. 108
80. Diagram of bee wing movement. 111
81. A forger collecting water from a flower pot drain hole. 113
82. The queen and her retinue. 116
83. A queen cell next to drone and worker cells. .117
84. Instrumental insemination of a honey bee queen. 118
85. Caged queens with attendant bees. 120
86. Doolittle queen production system layout. 121
87. Queen mating nuclei. 123
88. A full deep frame of honey. 127
89. Honey that has begun to granulate. 128
90. Bread made with honey and using creamed honey as a topping. 129
91. Three styles of honey dishes. 129
92. A polariscope, refractometer and color grader. 130
93. A honey exhibit at a bee meeting. 131
94. A forager coming in for a landing. 132
95. A full honey super. 133
96. A fume board used to remove honey supers. .134
97. Using a bee blower to remove bees from supers. 135
98. A modern hobby extracting setup. 136
99. Hand-held uncapping tools. 137
100. A generalized honey and wax processing sequence for the beginner. . . .138
101. A commercial honey bottling operation. 139
102. Cut-comb honey. 140
103. Full Ross Round™ honey frames. 141
104. Selling honey at a flea market. 142
105. A honey jar label. 143
106. A 2-queen honey production plan. 146
107. Tulip poplar, a primary nectar source in many areas. 148
108. Ornamental flowers, a common minor nectar source. 149
109. A honey bee pollen collector on dandelion. 150
110. Basic pollination procedures. 151
111. Pollen pellets in a pollen trap. 152
112. Rental hives in a commercial apple orchard. .153
113. A modern pollen trap. 155
114. Dry pollen substitute being fed to colonies in the early spring. 156
115. A brood frame infected with American foulbrood. 160
116. Terramycin being applied to a colony. 161
117. Burning equipment that was heavily infected with American foulbrood. 162
118. Larvae dying from European foulbrood. 163
119. Fecal streaking on the hive exterior caused by Nosema. 164
120. A Sacbrood infected larvae. 165

121. A Varroa mite. 165
122. A ventral view of a Varroa mite showing its specialized legs. 166
123. An Apistan® strip partially in place. A grease patty, used to control
     tracheal mites, is near the rear of the hive. 166
124. An electron scan of three adult tracheal mites within a worker bee's
     respiratory system. 167
125. Larval and adult stages of the Small Hive Beetle. 168
126. An adult Small Hive Beetle in the hive. The beetles are not large. 169
127. Fire ant mounds near the beehive. 170
128. Combs destroyed by wax moth larvae. 171
129. A mouse nest in a wintering beehive. 173
130. Beekeepers surrounded by Africanized honey bees. 175
131. Bees killed by an insecticide. 177
132. Cakes of rendered beeswax. 180
133. A solar wax melter. 181
134. High quality beeswax candles. 182
135. Propolis deposits along the edge of the hive body and on frame edges. 184
136. Two propolis traps—a wooden block and a plastic grid. 185
137. An observation hive in the Auburn University arboretum. 186
138. An observation hive on display. 188
139. Bottles of commercially brewed mead (honey wine). 190
140. An antique hive and skep with a woven super. 194
141. A shop-built bee vacuum device. 196
142. A slatted rack resting on a bottom board. 199
143. The slatted rack concept. 200
144. A drip board. 201

Beekeeping Principles

A Manual for the Beginner
A Guide for the Gardener

CHAPTER 1

Is Beekeeping for You?
An Overview of Bees and Beekeepers

The Life and Management of the Honey Bee in Review. The little honey bee is a tiny, energetic marvel. Raising brood, producing honey and pollinating plants are all in a day's work. In a worker bee's entire lifetime of 3–5 weeks, she will produce approximately 1/12 teaspoon of honey.

Figure 1. Honey bee forager on holly.

For a single bee to produce one pound of honey, she must visit two million blossoms to get enough nectar for the task. That same one pound jar of honey requires the equivalent of three trips around the world. The honey bee, ever efficient, uses only one ounce of honey of fuel for each orbit.

Worker bees are sterile females. The queen, the sole reproductive female, lays all the eggs, while worker bees do the other chores within the hive and never mate with drones. In addition, it is only female bees that sting. The male bees, or drones, only function is to provide reproductive services to unmated queens. The mating procedure results in the drone's death.

The bees' diet is very restricted. They use flower nectar (honey) as a carbohydrate source, while pollen, also collected from blossoms, is used as the protein source in their diets, nothing else. Some plants encourage insects (including honey bees) to visit their blossoms so pollen can be transferred from one flower to another. As pollen is transferred from one blossom to another within the same species, cross-pollination results, thus a higher quality and a greater quantity of many plant foods are produced.

Plants encourage bee visitation by offering nectar and pollen as a reward, or bribe, to a foraging bee. Many plants vie for foraging bee visits and offer different quality and quantity combinations of pollen and nectar. One could actually say that a foraging honey bee is much like a shopper in a grocery store. The thrifty bee is always looking for the best food values offered by plant blossoms.

Honey bees were surviving quite well long before there were beekeepers. In some instances, honey bees could probably survive better without the beekeeper's assistance. So what function does the beekeeper fulfill?

Figure 2. Two beekeepers working a hive.

The beekeeper keeps bees in hives that allow honey processing to be mechanized, clean, efficient, and disease free. The beekeeper hopes that the bees will produce more honey than the 60 pounds per year that each hive needs for its own use. If the bees have a good year, the beekeeper removes surplus honey. This is the sweetener that is on grocer's shelves. Maintaining disease free, productive gentle bees are the goal of adept beekeepers. Moreover, the production of a tasteful, pure honey crop is the end reward of the bees' and the beekeeper's combined efforts.

The different combinations of plant blossoms visited by bees determine the taste of the honey crop produced. If one feels that a particular honey taste is not pleasant, then another should be tried. The taste of honey varies, just as the flavors among different types of ice cream.

Honey bees are certainly an ally of United States of America (USA) agriculture. Honey production and blossom pollination are the life's work of the little honey bee. Without the efforts of the honey bee, fruits, melons, vegetables, ornamental plants, and wildlife foodstuffs would all suffer yield and seed reductions.

Is Beekeeping for You? Anyone, of either sex, at any age, can keep bees nearly anywhere. Beekeepers have no typical physical appearance, yet they must enjoy nature and not be overly fearful of insects, not just stinging insects. It is true that beekeepers suffer the occasional sting. It is painful, but not unbearable. In fact, for most beekeepers the enjoyment of micro-livestock husbandry and contributing to environmental systems, far outweigh the pain of the occasional sting. Protective equipment has been developed to completely protect the beekeeper.

A few hives of bees can be kept anywhere—even within large cities. Beehives have been kept on the roofs or balconies of city buildings as well as rural settings. Honey crops can be made anywhere in the USA.

The Beekeeping Craft. Beekeeping is an old craft that has been practiced for hundreds of years by people around the world. Current beekeeping practices are a combination of both antiquated and modern procedure. Science continually adds to the understanding of honey bee biology and behavior. The need for competent beekeepers is greater than ever due to the drastic loss of wild honey bee populations worldwide caused by predacious mites.

Figure 3. Beekeepers learning to work a hive (circa 1920).

CHAPTER 2

The Beekeeper's Equipment

The Simple Principle of Bee Space

The principle of bee space is the backbone of beekeeping. Prior to the development of this concept bees would either glue all the inside appliances with propolis (bee glue) or they would jam everything with burr comb. This resulted in a hive that could not be opened without destroying and traumatizing the colony.

Reverend Langstroth is credited with describing and implementing bee space principles. Simply, though critical, bee space requirements are: 1/4" and less will be filled with propolis while any measurement greater than 3/8" will be filled with comb. *The space between 1/4" and 3/8" will be left open.* Therefore, throughout the colony (all around the frames, between the bottom board and the frame bottoms, and the small space beneath the inner cover and frame top bars) bee space will be within 1/4"–3/8" and essentially stay free from propolis and wax. Whether buying or building beekeeping equipment, it is imperative that the concept of bee space is respected.

Bee Space Measurements

1/4" and less = Propolis filling
1/4" - 3/8" = Open space
3/8" and greater = Comb filling

Figure 4. Bee space measurements.

For comparison, humans require something similar to bee space. The ceilings in homes are of standard height, as are room sizes of bathrooms, bedrooms, and living rooms, even closets. The doors and windows within those rooms are also of a standard dimension. Automobiles are of similar sizes as is furniture. Change any of these dimensions, either larger or smaller, and standard human space is offended.

The beekeeper's equipment can be divided into two broad categories: hive equipment and protective clothing and equipment. Both types of equipment are necessary to the beekeeper.

Bee Hive Equipment

The commonly used standard bee hive is delightfully simple. At its core, it is made up of a rectangular wooden box. This box doesn't have a top or a bottom, only two sides and two ends. Within this basic box, ten frames are suspended from a ledge (called a rabbet) that has been cut inside the top edge of the box.

Figure 5. Standard beehive with two hive bodies and a telescoping outer cover.

The bees will build comb on beeswax foundation within the frames hanging from the ledges. The box with ten frames is then placed onto a bottom board and covered with a top. These few parts make up a small, simple bee hive. Though this hive is simple in design, there is more to know as the hive grows.

All standard bee hives are comprised of several basic parts, all having individual names. Many times in beekeeping, pieces of equipment are named for their location and purpose within the hive. Consequently, the same piece of equipment may have a couple of different names depending on where it is used within the hive. Starting from the bottom up, all common parts of the standard bee hive are discussed in the following sections.

The Hive Stand. In order to prevent back injury and to keep the bee colony from being in contact with the cold, damp soil, the hive should be raised off the ground.

Parts of A Modern Hive

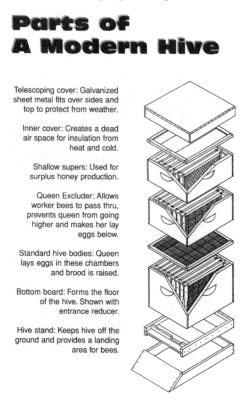

Telescoping cover: Galvanized sheet metal fits over sides and top to protect from weather.

Inner cover: Creates a dead air space for insulation from heat and cold.

Shallow supers: Used for surplus honey production.

Queen Excluder: Allows worker bees to pass thru, prevents queen from going higher and makes her lay eggs below.

Standard hive bodies: Queen lays eggs in these chambers and brood is raised.

Bottom board: Forms the floor of the hive. Shown with entrance reducer.

Hive stand: Keeps hive off the ground and provides a landing area for bees.

Figure 6. Parts of the standard hive.[1]

There are no perfect hive stands—but hives should be set on something. Bottom boards in direct contact with the ground will rot faster. In addition, low colonies are more likely to be harassed by nightly visits from skunks or other varmints. Common cement blocks are an all-time favorite, but they are too low and a bit too narrow. However, leave the colony too low to the ground and it will require constant back bending to work frames in the brood chamber. If there are several hives sitting on a common stand, all colonies will be disturbed when a single colony is worked. Commercially produced hive stands are okay, but have faults as well. They will decay and provide an excellent place for mice to spend the winter. Old tires, wooden beams, rocks, cement blocks, bed frames, or a two-seater abandoned out-door privy have been used for hive stands. Although the hive only needs to be off the ground a few inches, beekeepers frequently raise it to about 24" to 28". Much higher and it will be hard to lift supers to the top of the colony. Additionally, any lower will require a constant stoop when working the hive.

---

[1]Figure used with the permission of Rossman Apiaries, Moultrie, GA 31768

The Bottom Board. The bottom board is nothing more than a flat board surface with a lip on three sides. The board is the same width as the bee hive, but is about three inches longer. On one side, there is a 3/4" x 3/4" wooden rim on both edges and one end of the board. On the other side, there is a 3/8" x 3/4" wooden rim. Therefore, when the hive body is set on the bottom board, it is raised 3/4". The end of the bottom board, which has no rim, remains open and serves as the hive entrance. During the winter months, the bottom board is reversed and the shallower side is used. The 3/8" entrance is used to keep out mice during cold months.

Figure 7. A "reversible bottom board" with the 3/4" side up and the 3/8" side down.

Figure 8. An entrance reducer.

The Entrance Reducer. Rather than flip the bottom board to the shallow side, many beekeepers choose to leave the bottom board on the deep side year-round and install an entrance reducer instead. An entrance reducer restricts the entrance to a small opening that excludes most intruders, such as mice. The advantage to using an entrance reducer is that to be installed the hive does not have to be torn down to the bottom board.

The Brood Chamber. Essentially, the brood chamber is the hive's living room and is the heart of the hive. The queen, brood and most of the bees live here. Commonly, the brood chamber is made up of two deep hive bodies, providing abundant room for prolific queens to lay eggs. Though costing more initially, using two hive bodies rather than one greatly increases the beekeeper's management options. Procedures such as making splits, reversing brood chambers for spring build-up and swarm control are some of the reasons for keeping a strong colony in double hive bodies.

The Queen Excluder. The queen excluder is a metal grid framed with a thin wooden rim. Its measurements are exactly those of the hive bodies, so it fits flush on all sides when in use on the colony. The limiting space between individual grids allows worker bees to pass, but will prohibit the larger queen beyond the excluder. Drones are also unable to pass through an excluder. The excluder is placed between the brood nest and the supers. When working properly, the queen will be confined to the brood nest and will not be able to put brood in the honey supers. Having brood in supers is not necessarily bad from the standpoint of honey quality. The problem is that brood needed by the colony is lost and, on some occasions, even the queen is lost if she is accidentally removed from the colony in a super.

Figure 9. Various types of queen excluders.

Seemingly, from the time queen excluders were introduced until now, there have been on-going debates as to their usefulness. Many beekeepers feel that heavily-loaded returning bees have difficulty squeezing through the device therefore reducing the honey crop. Even if a bit of the crop is lost, it is generally a good idea for inexperienced beekeepers to use the device. It makes the honey crop removal much simpler.

For a number of years queen excluders were also made of punched zinc or plastic. While both of these styles work reasonably well, they require more care in handling. In fact, any queen excluder requires careful handling. If the spacing between the grids is even slightly damaged, the queen will find it and put brood in the honey supers. Excluders should be removed from the colony when they are not needed.

Honey Supers. Supers are honey storage boxes separated from the brood chambers by the queen excluder (if one is used). During times of surplus honey production, and after filling the brood nest, foraging bees will store honey in supers for later use.

Supers come in several different sizes. Obviously, when filled with honey, the deeper supers are heavier than the shallower supers. A deep hive body can be used either as a brood chamber or as a deep super. Some beekeepers like the convenience of a single depth box for use as both super and hive bodies and will use that particular style throughout the hive. However, using the smaller supers for brood chambers will increase the hive's initial cost.

The Inner Cover. The inner cover is a companion piece of equipment to a telescoping outer cover (discussed below). As with other pieces

Figure 10. A Porter Bee Escape in the handhold of an inner cover.

of bee equipment, its name varies depending on how it is used. Normally it is positioned with its deep side up during warm months. This maintains correct bee space. However, during cold months when bees cannot produce honey or wax, the inner cover is positioned with the deep side down. This gives the bees more cluster space on the frame top bars. Occasionally beekeepers use a *bee escape* in the inner cover handhold to devise a simple *escape board*. This inner cover/bee escape device goes between the brood chamber and honey supers. It is used to free the supers of bees.

During warm months, the space provided between the inner cover and outer cover is much like the attic in a house. It aids in heat control. More importantly is that the inner cover prevents the bees from gluing the outer cover to the hive with propolis. Inner covers make opening a colony with a telescoping outer cover much easier.

Inner covers are made of wood, plastic, or Masonite®. Though any type of inner cover does a good job, most beekeepers prefer wooden ones. Many older inner covers, and some new ones, have a semi-circular notch cut in one end of the wooden rim. This opening serves as an upper entrance during both warm and cold months. The outer cover can be pushed against the inner cover to close the upper entrance. In addition the outer cover may be moved slightly away from the inner cover to open the upper entrance.

Figure 11. The inner cover with the deep side up.

The Outer Cover. The outer cover is simply a roof for the hive. It may be nothing more than a flat board. It may have a wooden rim (about 2 inches deep) around all four edges of the top to form a lip. The rim allows the top to telescope over the sides and ends of the top super. The telescoping cover is commonly covered with a sheet of galvanized tin, making it quite heavy. It requires an inner cover to prevent the bees from gluing the outer cover to the top super. Consequently, the telescoping outer cover costs considerably more than a flat board cover.

The flat board outer cover normally has a shallow cleat on both ends, but not on the sides. Since it is possible to insert a hive tool in the side crack formed between the side of the top super and the outer cover, flat board covers do not require an inner cover.

Ironically, both styles of outer covers have the same problem. That is, they will blow off the hive in a gusty wind. Though crudely effective, many beekeepers place a rock or cement block on top of the hive to keep the cover in place.

Identifying Hive Equipment.

Many beekeepers purchase a distinctive brand and mark their equipment with a burned mark. Branding should be done before the equipment is painted. However, it can be done after many coats of paint have been applied. Brands have been useful on many occasions in the past, when hives were stolen or equipment was mixed between several honey producers. The initial cost of the branding head and brand are quite costly. They must be ordered from bee supply companies or from specialty suppliers.

Figure 12. A nice brood frame from a branded hive body.

Assembling the Bee Hive.

In order to save shipping costs, beehive equipment is shipped unassembled. The assembly process is a common aspect of beekeeping and can be quite enjoyable.

The tools and facilities required to assemble the hive are not complicated. Tools that may be needed include a claw hammer, square, stout worktable, water repellent glue, pencil and a pair of pliers.

Figure 13. Assemble hive body with the handholds to the outside.

Figure 14. Attaching rails to the bottom board.

Figure 15. Box joints in the hive body. Note pre-drilled nail holes.

The assembly of the major hive components is straightforward. A common error in assembly of the hive body or super is that the handle notches are placed inside rather than outside the hive body. The equipment will come with cement-coated nails of appropriate sizes.

Before assembly, lay out the parts of the bottom board. The tongue & groove boards fit in the groove cut into the side rails. Backstops of 3/4 inch and 3/8 inch are used to close the back of the bottom board. Although it would be helpful to have three hands, it goes together logically.

Some parts of the outer cover, inner cover, supers and hive bodies are pre-drilled for nails. Be sure to use the correct nail size. Instructions and nails are included.

Rather than using nails, a few beekeepers are using galvanized coated screws. Future repairs can be easily made on the equipment whereas cross nailing the joint makes future repairs virtually impossible.

Painting the Bee Hive.

Latex paint is highly recommended for painting the outer surfaces of the hive. The insides of both the bottom board, the insides of all brood chambers and supers as well as the inside of the outer cover are left unpainted. The inner cover is left unpainted. If wood preservatives are used, they should be applied only to outer surfaces and materials approved for bee hive use. High-grade penetrating oils, such as Penetrol®, have been shown to be effective when used as an undercoat for exterior paints. Dipping wooden equipment in hot paraffin or beeswax mixed with rosin has been popular. All hive surfaces, including inside surfaces, can be protected. It is quite simple to re-dip as needed. This procedure requires a large vat of very hot molten wax. It is important to take precautions, since hot splashes and spills are common.

Figure 16. A hive with both painted and paraffin-dipped hive bodies.

For the most part, the color of the paint is irrelevant. It is common for beekeepers to color-code their equipment. At a glance, one can tell what type of super is on the colony. White is the most common beehive color. Black paint is not recommend due to heat absorption.

Figure 17. A colorful Australian beehive. Note the clip for hooking the hive together and the permanently-mounted entrance reducer.

Frame Assembly and Foundation Installation

Frame assembly is the "finish carpentry" of the hive assembly process. Frame assembly can be tedious. The frame is comprised of a top bar, two end bars, and a bottom bar of some type. The 3/4" wedge-type top bar has always been the most common. The end bars have scalloped edges halfway up their length, to allow the bees easier movement around frame ends. On many end bars, both upper edges on one side are chamfered or beveled while the edges on the opposite side of the same end bar are left square. The chamfered edges should be on opposite sides and opposite ends of the top bar from each other. In this way, on the same side of the top bar, a beveled edged side is paired with a square-edged end bar on the other end. This sounds much more confusing than it is. Beveling the edges on one side of the end bar helps the beekeeper keep the bees from gluing the end bars together when in the colony.

Figure 18. End bar attachment showing beveled upper edges.

Propolis, the bees' natural caulking and gluing compound, historically, has been a major problem for beekeepers. Excessive use of propolis makes a hive essentially impossible to open. Any help the beekeeper can get by using such aids as inner covers or beveled edges on end bars is a welcomed relief during colony manipulations. Having said all that, it is not a requirement that the edges of the end bars be beveled. If necessary, they can be beveled with a hand plane or sander.

There are a variety of bottom bars that can be a bit trying also. The common types are: solid, grooved, split and two-pieced bottom bars. The most common style is two-piece, but be certain that the bottom bars are compatible with the end bars when ordering.

Figure 19. Solid, grooved, split and two-piece bottom bars.

Frame Assembly. Attach the end bars to the top bar with 1-1/2" nails that are provided with the frames. Nailing on a solid surface helps keep the nail from bending. Use glue and be certain that the end bar bevels are on different sides of the top bar. Be consistent by putting the left thumb on the top bar wedge and right thumb on one of the beveled edges of the end bar. Holding the parts in that position, attach the end bar to the top bar using glue and nails. Use two nails per each end bar. Flip the frame end-for-end and attach the opposite end bar to the top bar. Lay the frame on the top bar and attach the bottom bars—again using glue and

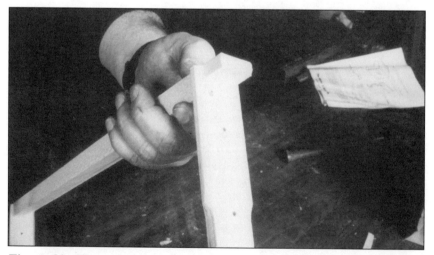

Figure 20. The correct position of the end bar nail near the beekeeper's thumb.

nails. The process is finished at this point, but many beekeepers place one more nail through the end bar to make the joint stronger. A 1-1/4" nail is driven through the side of the end bar into the thick part of the top bar. Though it is somewhat difficult to do, once the side nail is in place, the frame is sturdily glued and cross-nailed. Do not plan to make too many repairs on this frame in the future, however. It will be nearly impossible to remove the end bars from the top bars. After the frame is glued and nailed, but before the glue dries, visually check it for squareness. If it is out of square (and it usually is), gently rack the frame into square.

A few things may help with frame assembly. If nailing is challenging, drill pilot holes in the frame parts. Pilot holes are drilled in many parts of the hive, but are not drilled in frame parts. Pneumatic or electric brad drivers are great when used to assemble frames. However, since brads have small heads, be sure to use glue in conjunction with the nails. Wear safety glasses. Nailing jigs are quite handy for holding ten frames at once for all assembly other than the end bar side nails, but are not required.

Plastic Frames. In recent years, plastic frames have increased in popularity. There is no assembly required and in most cases, the price is competitive with wooden frames. Plastic frames do not have the rigidity of wooden frames and bees may be more reluctant to accept them. The major advantage is that they save considerable time in assembly of the frame and the installation of foundation. Overall, plastic frames hold considerable promise for the time-strapped bee-keeper.

Figure 21. A selection of plastic frames.

Installing Foundation. Though beeswax-coated plastic sheets are widely accepted, many beekeepers still use "wired" foundation. During the process of frame assembly, notice the drilled holes in the end bars. A single strand of small gauge wire, attached at one end with a nail on one of the end bars, is passed back and forth through the holes. The wire is pulled taunt, but not piano-string tight. After being passed through the end bar holes, the wire is wrapped several times around a second nail in the opposite end bar. The second nail is then driven home and the wire is broken off. The thin, strong wire will easily cut the wooden end bars. The holes for the wire have brass or aluminum "eyelets" pushed into the holes before the wire is threaded through. Normally, frames are only wired horizontally. Pre-wired foundation comes with vertical wires.

The wedge in the top bar, held in place by a thin sliver of wood, is broken out and laid aside. A sheet of wired foundation, with hooks turned upward in the notch left by the wedge, is laid on the wires. The wedge is repositioned and tacked back onto the top bar, thereby trapping the foundation wire ends underneath the wedge. On the bottom bar side of the frame, the foundation sheet slips into the slit between the two bottom bars. At this point, the foundation is only held in place by the wedge. While giving support from beneath with a shallow board cut to size, the wires are imbedded into the foundation either by a "spur wire embedder" or by using an electric wire-embedder. Looking like a pizza cutter with a notched cutter wheel, the spur embedder simply pushes the wire into the foundation while the electric embedder melts the wire into the foundation. Either works acceptably.

Figure 22. An electric wire-embedding setup. The wire embedder is lying in front of the stand.

Many beekeepers use various time- and labor-saving tactics when building and installing foundation. Probably the greatest convenience is beeswax-coated plastic foundation. It does not require any wiring or subsequent embedding. On occasion however, the bees reject such foundation if there is no nectar flow.

No matter which type of foundation is used, it should be straight when finished. The quality of the future comb depends on the straightness of the installed foundation.

The Beekeeper's Protective Equipment

Beekeeping is a craft of many highly visible trademarks. The white hive and the antique-looking smoker are certainly well-known, but best known of all is the characteristic veil and the protective clothing that the beekeeper wears when working bees. A review of the protective equipment section of current bee supply catalogs shows a variety of veils, gloves and protective suits. Prices for such equipment varies widely.

Figure 23. Two fully-protected beekeepers working a populous hive. Note the smoker and hive stand.

The Beekeeper's Veil. No matter how long one has been keeping bees, a sting around the nose, eyes or lips gives the beekeeper a real wake-up call. Normally, the veil is held away from the face a few inches and is either attached or tied to the beekeeper's suit. Veils are made of plastic screen or blackened screen wire. It is best to use the screen wire types for heavy use and the plastic screen veils for lighter use. Regardless of which one is used, it is important that a veil of some kind is always worn. A sting around the eyes can be outright dangerous.

The Bee Suit. Beginning beekeepers often wear a full-length suit, gloves and a veil. Though completely protected from stings, the suited beekeeper is exposed to extreme heat in warm or hot weather. Many will eliminate the suit in favor of a half suit or will only wear heavy street clothes. It is recommended to keep a full wardrobe of protective clothing on hand and wear as much as necessary. Some days the bees are more defensive than other days. Gloves are helpful and will protect from stings, but they can also cause clumsiness. The amount of protective clothing required depends on the expertise of the beekeeper and the extent of the current task that must be accomplished. For instance, searching for queens or removing supers from an entire yard would require a heavy suit. Alternatively, opening a colony for a quick look would require minimal clothing. It depends on the bees' attitude on the day the hives are being worked.

The Smoker and Its Use

Beekeepers have used various forms of smokers for many years. Their form and design have changed, but the basic function has not. That function is to produce copious amounts of billowy white smoke. Smoke, when puffed into the colony, will mask the bees' chemical communication system thus allowing the beekeeper a protected moment to perform various beekeeping procedures. It is important that the smoke be cool. Hot smoke will damage the bees' wings and make them hostile. In addition, a little smoke goes a long way. There is no need to have the entire hive fogged in smoke. Just a couple of puffs at the entrance and a couple on top of the frames will allow entry into the colony. The bees will be actively buzzing to dissipate the smoke. After about 2–5 minutes, the bees will begin to recover from the first smoke application and more smoke

Figure 24. A beekeeper smoking a hive.

should be administered. When does the colony need more smoke? When the bees begin to line back up in orderly fashion along the top bars and when the bees are becoming "flighty" and are striking the gloves.

Smoker Fuels. Nearly anything can be a smoker fuel as long as it will produce white, cool smoke. Paper generally burns too fast. Materials such as untreated burlap, pine needles, dry leaves, punk wood, dried cow manure, wheat chaff, sumac pods, and wood shavings are some examples of common smoker fuels. Pine needles are a good choice as a dependable fuel. Pine needles are free, have a nice aroma, and light easily, but the smoker will need frequent repacking when pine needles are used as the fuel. Mixing pine needles with wood shavings will extend the life of the fire. Do not use anything that has been treated with pesticides or that has any other chemical residue.

Lighting the Smoker. Techniques used for lighting smokers vary with the specific fuels used. Even so, when lighting a smoker, use something easily ignitable such as paper or leaves. Get a good flame coming out of the pot. Lightly sprinkle more fuel into the flame until it fades. Puff the smoker vigorously until the flame reappears. Add more fuel and repeat the process. At this stage, a coal bed is developing in the smoker. After about three cycles, begin to fuel the smoker much more tightly— but bring it back either to a flame or to easy smoke each time. Finally, pack the smoker tightly, and intermittently give the bellows a good pumping to keep the coals alive. Many beekeepers feel that laying the smoker on its side when not in use keeps the coals hotter for a longer time.

The Hive Tool

In other worlds, the common hive tool is sold as a window opener. Essentially, the hive tool is a small pry-bar with a broad, flat spatula-type end. The hooked end of the hive tool is used for scraping wax and propolis

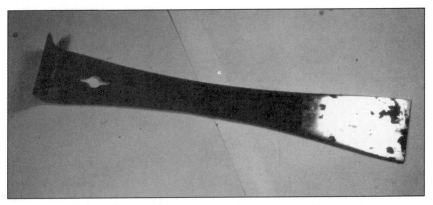

Figure 25. The common, indispensable hive tool.

from the hive and frames. The spatula end is used for prying out frames or opening the colony. Hive tools do a great job, but are easily lost or forgotten. Screwdrivers are frequently pressed into service, but are not well-suited as hive tools. Do not over-stress the tool and keep the hook end reasonably sharp. With a little care, one tool can easily last an entire beekeeping career.

CHAPTER 3

Buying Existing Colonies of Honey Bees

Purchasing an existing hive of honey bees is a commonly-accepted way to begin beekeeping. Buying an established hive is much like buying a used car. There are good ones and bad ones.

When buying an established colony, check:
1. The health and strength of the colony
2. The standardization of the equipment
3. The amount of honey currently on the colony
4. The physical appearance of equipment
5. How far the colony will need to be moved
6. How much equipment goes with each hive
7. The selling price of the hive

Advantages of Purchasing Established Colonies. The advantages to buying existing colonies are obvious. The equipment is already assembled and painted. The comb is already drawn, the queen is already in place and, during warmer months, brood is being produced. In essence, an inexperienced individual is suddenly responsible for a large honey bee colony.

Disadvantages of Purchasing Established Colonies. Although all manufactured equipment is somewhat standard, it is not precisely standardized. While mixed equipment will work compatibly, it will result in increased levels of propolization and burr comb production. If the price is right the shortcoming will not be a serious problem. However, if the adult population is strong, as it should be, the novice beekeeper will suddenly find that he or she must quickly be an adept hive manager. The colony weight, the number of stings, and the number of management expectations are all greater than the expectations from a newly-begun colony. Most importantly, a novice beekeeper would be least trained to recognize common bee diseases and pests.

Colony Health. Since colony health is very important, the new beekeeper should get help determining the physical health of a colony. Many times, the local bee inspector, or another competent beekeeper, can determine the health status of the colony. Many states can review the seller's bee disease history. The new beekeeper should have someone check the colony's well-being before purchasing. American foulbrood can be devastating to a new beekeeper's project.

Equipment Condition. If the equipment is not standardized or if it shows signs of rot or serious disrepair, the selling price should be reduced. Equipment in poor condition will offset advantages posed by the equipment already being assembled.

Colony Population. Again, unless the selling price is attractive, the colony population should be high. Remember that wintering colonies are at their lowest population but will quickly build up assuming the presence of a productive queen, adequate honey stores, and the absence of common bee hive pests. In general, do not purchase colonies in winter months unless stipulations are attached or unless the purchaser knows the seller.

Colony Location. The purchaser must consider the distance the colony will need to be moved. The greater the moving distance, the greater the potential for problems. However, this will have to be an individual decision.

Selling Price. Selling prices for hives have been erratic since Varroa mites systematically killed so many colonies. A hypothetical hive, in early spring, that is strong (abundant bees in both deeps) with two deeps, both of which are in good condition, in early spring has potential for producing a honey crop or pollination rental. Such a hive, depending on a host of variables, would sell for $75–$150 (year 2000 price). Anything less is approaching a bargain, while anything greater than $150 would need to have special considerations[2]. Colonies going into winter might be somewhat less expensive as would colonies being purchased after the spring nectar flow had ended.

In general, a new beekeeper would be okay purchasing a colony in late winter or early spring as long as the colony was certified disease-free and as long as the new beekeeper has access to beekeeping expertise from another source.

Figure 26. Good colonies for purchasing. Note good population and good equipment condition.

---

[2]J.E. Tew personal estimation

CHAPTER 4

Starting Hives from Package Bees

Package Bees

Getting started in beekeeping with package bees is a common procedure. Package bee operations are specifically designed to produce honey bees, and not honey, as the crop. There are several advantages to starting with packages. First, unlike acquiring a swarm, it provides some idea of when the bees will arrive. Secondly, rather than buying a large, established hive, the new beekeeper's expertise can grow as the new beehive grows. A disadvantage is that the cost of packages has risen and will probably continue to increase slowly. Additionally shipping costs are rising rapidly.

Figure 27. Packages of bees ready for shipment from a southern producer.

Ordering Packages. When ordering packages, placing a phone call to the producer is a good idea. Be prepared to talk about several things. First, package sizes, ordering dates and prices. The most common package size is three pounds though two- and five-pound packages are occasionally sold. Larger packages should build up more quickly, but would also cost more. Shipping dates are important. Too early and the bees will chill after being released but too late and much of the spring season will have already passed. Most customers have a date range (e.g. the week of April 20th—not the day of April 20th) rather than requesting a specific day. Placing orders in September before the next spring is common. Choose a trusted package producer. Most package producers value their customers highly. It is not always possible to order packages early. Sometimes plans change due to beekeeping reasons. Just as one can frequently get tickets to a sold-out ball game or get a ticket on a full airplane, a beekeeper can sometimes get packages late in the season due to another beekeeper's cancellation. Both the customer and the producer are uncertain. The customer is estimating how many packages will be needed next spring and the producer is guessing how many packages can be shaken and sold next spring. The weather can change everything. Employees become ill or take other employment or the customer has a greater winterkill than expected. Some years, things just do not go well. Be flexible when ordering, but it is a good idea to order early. In general, have the packages arrive about a week or so before fruit bloom in most areas. Another suggestion is to order an extra queen per every ten packages or so. Hold them in other colonies or in cages in new package bee colonies. Extra queens are cheap insurance. If the queens cannot be used immediately, another beekeeper will be happy to have them.

The payment method for the packages will surely come up during conversations with the package producer. Every company has different expectations. Some will require a non-refundable deposit (applied to the purchase price), while others do not. If a significant number of package bees are ordered, as much as half of the selling price may be required up front. How will the remainder be covered? Again, for smaller orders, certified money orders or other types of secured payment exchange may be requested. For shipping purposes, there are two options: the U.S. Postal Service or traveling to the producer's location. Each year it is rumored that UPS will begin accepting package shipments, but that has not happened yet. Occasionally, an order can be combined with those of other beekeepers in the area and result in a reduced shipping price.

Holding Packages until Installation. It is a good idea to get the bees out of the package soon after arrival, but sometimes this is not possible. To maintain bees mix a solution of thin sugar syrup and spray the mixture on the sides of the cage. Store packages in a dark room that is around 50–55°F. A dark cool basement is a possibility. Spray the packages several times per day; then leave them alone. If the bees must be held longer than three days, lay the package on its side and put a feeder can directly on the screen. The shipping can is assumed to be empty. When bees are installed after being confined for that long, be prepared for extensive bee defecation droppings upon their release.

Package Installation. The procedure for installing packages is deceptively simple. Spray the packages with thin sugar syrup until mid afternoon (roughly 50% water and 50% sugar). Plan to install the bees toward late afternoon. Have all hive equipment ready. Remove the center four frames from the brood chamber. Next, using the tip of the hive tool, remove the top cover from the package exposing the feeder can and the top of the queen cage. Firmly bounce the bees down within the cage. Knowing that the procedure will greatly annoy the bees, this process bothers many new beekeepers. Though occasional stings do occur, there should be minimal stinging if the bees have been well fed. Before all the bees can recover from the bouncing, deftly remove the feeder can, remove the queen cage, and then quickly, but temporarily, lay the cover on the cage to prohibit bees escaping. At this point, bees are flying all about and confusion seems to be increasing, but that is normal. Visually determine that the queen is alive, and then, by removing the cork expose the candy plug on the queen cage. (Note: Some packages may have a plastic queen cage. The instructions for release are similar.) Place the prepared queen cage nearby. Holding the temporarily-repositioned package lid, give the package a second bump, jar the bees to the bottom of the cage, and then pour and shake the bees into the brood chamber space left by removing the four frames. At this point, bees are really flying everywhere—but most are in a heap within the brood chamber. Gently replace about three of the frames and using thumb tacks or thin wire, attach the queen cage with the wire tie that comes with the queen cage in the middle of the developing cluster. Be careful to keep the open side of the queen cage facing outward in order for worker bees to have access to the cage. Note that the queen cage within the hive will probably require temporarily leaving one frame out. Shake the few remaining bees in front of the colony and watch for them to begin scenting. This is an indication that they have recognized the colony entrance. Get the empty package away from the colony. Put a feeder on the colony and close it up. It is a good idea to reduce the entrance down to about one inch. At this point, do not do anything for a couple of days except refill the sugar feeder. About three days later, quickly open the colony and release the queen if she is not already out. If a frame had to be left, replace it at this time. After releasing the queen, do not disturb the hive for about a week to fill the feeder.

Figure 28. Shaking bees from a package. Note the caged queen ready for installation.

Figure 29. Bees from a recently-released package.

One variation could be considered. Rather than pouring the bees from the cage, set the open package in the open space within the colony. A second full deep hive body with frames is then placed above the package and the hive closed up. Rather than being shaken out, the bees should slowly move out of the package into the upper hive body. However, sometimes they do not want to leave the shipping package still requiring them to be shaken out. A couple of days later remove both package and queen cages at once. Either way, it is not difficult. Just get the bees out of the package one way or another.

CHAPTER 5

Hiving Swarms

For many years, swarm retrieval was a common way that people got into beekeeping or increased their colony numbers each spring. Many times, they were swarms from their own hives, but frequently beekeepers would be called to remove swarms from the property of non-beekeepers. One of the most spectacular swarm removals was on television many years ago. A beekeeper was called to remove the swarm from a commercial television camera that was being used to broadcast a major-league baseball game. The beekeeper was a hero that day.

When Swarms Leave. Swarms can depart the hive nearly anytime during warm months but, by far, most swarms leave the parent colony during the springtime. Swarms usually leave during midday, but they can leave at nearly any time if the weather is nice. Swarms were common before Varroa mites became established. Now most swarms are from the apiaries of managed bees, usually from the beekeeper's own hives.

Swarm Composition. Swarms are made up of a cross section of the parent hive bees. They average in size from that of a baseball to that of a basketball. There are bees of every type (foragers, guards, nurse bees, and comb builders) found in the new swarm. After taking full loads of honey into their internal storage containers (the crop), roughly half the bees in the colony issue with the swarm. Although frequently, many give up the adventure and return to the parent colony. The swarm moves along, like a living fog, until it settles on something. There is no statistical indication that the swarm is looking for a particular landing site. It appears to be a function of where the queen happens to randomly drop. Consequently, swarms may land on the ground or may set up camp high in a tree canopy. Though active swarms do not appear to be looking for any particular spot on which to settle, there is a clear indication that bee swarms are attracted to spots previously occupied by other swarms. Beekeepers having bees in established yards know where the hot spots are for swarms settling.

Hiving Swarms. Getting swarms to move into the empty hive is fairly easy. Swarms are normally gentle and are looking for a home. Bee equipment that has been previously used is highly attractive to a fresh swarm. Though shaking the bees into the equipment is frequently required, many times the bees will march in with little prodding from the beekeeper. Alternatively, if the swarm has hung on the same spot for several days, it may be more reluctant to give up the old home place. After bees have been shaken into the new equipment, they may doggedly return to the old spot. If possible, finding the queen, caging her, and putting her in the new equipment will usually force the swarm to move over to the empty equipment. However, it may take several hours before this happens. Throughout any of these procedures, the beekeeper should expect bees to be flying all around in a confused fashion. Many will return to the parent colony, but essentially the bees are looking for scent fields set up by bees that have found the new location. An indicator of success is how many bees are scenting on or near the new equipment.

Figure 30. A large prime swarm.

Since it takes several hours for all the bees to make the move to their new home, the beekeeper is usually required to return after dark to retrieve the new hive. If the colony is simply moved after most of the bees have gone in, remaining bees may re-cluster on the previous site and remain there for days —to the consternation of the homeowner. Other than possibly vacuuming the swarm rather than hiving it, there are few options open to the beekeeper.

In reality, beekeepers are frequently unprepared for the swarm call. Though swarms are particularly attracted to previously used equipment, nearly any box could suffice for the short term. Though it sounds a bit desperate, a few beekeepers have used their veils as bags for transporting swarms back to their home yard. If bees are carried in some unconventional box, be prepared to provide for ventilation. Large numbers of confined bees can suffocate rapidly.

Ask Some Questions First. Homeowners are usually happy to be rid of the swarm and view it as something dangerous. When receiving a call, ask the following questions:

1. *Are they truly honey bees?* Many times common wasps or yellowjackets are confused with honey bees.

2. *How long have they been there?* Swarms that have been in the same location for several days are referred to as "dry swarms" having used up all the temporary stores that they took with them. Such swarms can be surprisingly defensive and sting too much. In such cases, use a spray bottle filled with sugar syrup and spray the bees heavily several times before attempting to shake them into the bee equipment.
3. *How high off the ground are they?* Swarms that are particularly high are rarely worth the physical risk of climbing to get to them. Let them go on their own.
4. *Are they clustered in the open?* If the bees have gone into the wall of a house, for instance, they are no longer a swarm but are bees that will have to be physically removed from the house. Often, a few bees will cluster around the new entrance making the home-owner think that it is a hanging swarm.
5. *Are they yours to give away?* On occasion, the homeowner has a beekeeping neighbor who has let a swarm get away. Though technically the swarm no longer belongs to the original beekeeper, bad feelings could result if one is caught picking up another beekeeper's swarm.

No doubt during the conversation, the size of the swarm will be discussed. Extremely small swarms, baseball to softball sized, are frequently "secondary swarms" (also called afterswarms or mating swarms) and are headed by virgin queens. Such swarms, though hived the same way as regular swarms, are much more flighty and will quickly leave the site. The unmated queen that heads secondary swarms is quick to fly and is hard to find within the swarm body. In addition, since they are small, secondary swarms build up much more slowly than a full-sized (also called a prime) swarm. Primary swarms, those of full size and having a mated queen, are excellent comb builders and will build up quickly. A major reason for the impressive build-up is that the new swarm has no brood to feed; all gathered nectar goes directly to comb construction and to honey accumulation. Since the old queen always leaves with the swarm, and such intensive brood production is immediately required of her, new swarms frequently supersede the old queen during the same season that the swarm issued.

Controlling the swarming urge is difficult. Swarm initiation is the way in which bee colonies propagate themselves and is biologically driven. Two management schemes that will greatly reduce swarming are: (1) keeping a one- or two-year old queen as head of the colony and (2) giving ample space in both the brood nest and in the honey supers **long before** the colony requires the space. Once a colony has accepted the urge to swarm, little can be done to stop it. Occasionally, beekeepers destroy swarm cells to prevent swarming, but that is risky. Overlook just one and the swarm will go. Alternatively, if the swarm has already left, tearing down the queen cells will make the parent colony hopelessly queenless. Finally, colonies with a strong swarm drive will actually swarm without leaving any queen cells at all. The swarming characteristic is genetically derived. Each swarm retrieved will continue to add the swarming inclination to the beekeeper's operation. Again, frequent requeening will limit, but not eliminate swarms.

Bee Beards—Unique Swarms Hanging In Unique Places

Bee beards are nothing more than swarms that are placed on the face of a willing beekeeper. Bee beards are famous for attracting crowds at public outings. Opinions among beekeepers vary widely. Many beekeepers see bee beards as providing a novel opportunity to teach the public about the ease of bee handling and the gentleness of bees. Conversely, other beekeepers see bee beards as an exhibit approaching that of eating fire or handling snakes and feels that it does not leave beekeeping in a good light. This is something each beekeeper must decide.

Figure 31. A bee beard team.

Putting a Bee Beard On. All aspects of swarm management apply in the case of the bee beard. The bees, held in packages should be well fed and kept cool. Bees to be used in the demonstration should be shaken into shipping packages from the brood nest area of a gentle colony. It will take about 3–5 pounds of bees to make a well-defined beard.

The entire event should be within a large screened cage that is in good condition. It is suggested to position the cage on a trailer to allow people to see the procedure. The person on whom the beard is to be installed should be an experienced beekeeper who can take several stings without flinching. There is no place to hide once the procedure has begun. The beard wearer may choose to stuff his/her ears and nose with cotton swabs, thus breathing through the mouth. Generally, there is no protection for the eyes.

The Installation Process. An *Installer* (the individual who is responsible for releasing the bees and shaping them on the wearer) assists the *Wearer*. Two installers are preferable. Using a piece of twine and attaching the ends to the ears of the wearer, one installer ties the queen, that has been caged, under the neck of the wearer. The installer then uses a large piece of cardboard, having a semi-circular hole cut in one edge to accommodate the wearer. While the wearer holds the cardboard in place, the installer dumps the bees on the board near the caged queen. It is important to note that the bees have been fed with sugar syrup beforehand and may be misted just before the demonstration begins. Though many bees will take flight, most bees, being heavily laden with sugar syrup, will pile up on the board around the queen and on the face of the wearer. Using a credit card as a shaping tool, the installer shapes the swarm on the wearer's face, being careful to keep bees away from the wearer's eyes. Naturally, the bees should not be crushed against the face of the wearer. If all goes well, the bees will shape into a cluster surrounding the queen in about ten minutes. The wearer gently stands up and models the beard for the crowd. It is common for people to want to snap photos. After a few minutes, depending on the demeanor of the bees, the swarm is removed.

The Removal Process. The wearer leans over a large funnel, frequently improvised by rolling a piece of cardboard into an open cone. The wearer abruptly jerks his or her head thereby jarring most of the bees loose. They drop into the funnel and back into the package. The remaining bees on the wearer and within the demonstration cage are vacuumed into the shipping cage using a special vacuum trap. That prevents bees from being sucked into the vacuum tank. The caged queen is removed and placed in the package holding the bees. The removal process only takes a few minutes.

CHAPTER 6

The Annual Hive Management Cycle— An Overview

There are only two seasons for the beehive—spring and winter. Summer and fall are only extensions of spring and winter. The amount of time and effort that individual beekeepers have to allocate to their colony management varies greatly. Controlling parasitic mites and other infectious diseases is the task listed below that is critical. Comprehensive discussion of these points is in the following chapters.

Figure 32. Spring and winter bee hives at The Ohio State University Honey Bee Laboratory (Wooster, Ohio).

Major Annual Hive Management Tasks

1. In some legal way, chemically or managerially, control mites within the colony (fall and early spring, summer if necessary). This is critical.
2. Control swarming by preventing colony crowding (late spring and early summer).
3. Keep water in or near the hive (spring, summer, and fall).
4. Requeen every two years (during spring, summer, or fall).
5. Prevent robbing (spring, summer and fall).
6. Avoid high pesticide-use areas (spring, summer, and fall).
7. Protect the hive from temperature extremes—both heat and cold (winter and summer).
8. Keep mice out during winter months (fall and winter).
9. Regularly monitor and treat for other diseases, such as Nosema (annually).
10. Provide both sugar syrup and pollen supplements as needed (annually).

Minor Annual Hive Management Tasks

1. Protect colonies from ants (spring, summer and fall).
2. Equalize colonies within the same yard (spring, summer and fall).
3. Reverse the inner cover during cold months (fall and winter).
4. Do not set colonies directly on the ground (winter).
5. Protect the hive from night marauders such as skunks (annually).
6. Protect the colony from potential vandals (annually).
7. Only select apiary sites that have dependable access (annually).
8. Keep hive equipment standardized and in good maintenance (annually).
9. Constantly cull combs. Only use the best (annually).
10. Provide for hive ventilation (annually).

CHAPTER 7

Spring and Summer Management of Bee Colonies

Spring is the busiest time of the year for the beekeeper. The beekeeping management cycle is linked from one season to the next. Spring management depends on the fall and winter management of the previous year. In other words, what a beekeeper does during the previous fall and winter management scheme will directly affect what is needed in the upcoming spring.

Spring management can be divided into early spring and late spring. Spring management for honey production is more detailed than general spring management.

Early Spring

Check Honey Stores. Abundant honey stores are important to the early spring colony. If all other elements are in place, brood production is well underway, resulting in the appetites of developing brood making great demands on stored honey. Remember that, at this time of the year, there are no nectar sources on which bees can forage. Clusters are normally in the top deep. It is recommended to reposition honey stores nearer the cluster if not there already. Ideally, add frames of honey that were saved for this purpose. If colonies are light and full honey frames are not available to give to the colonies, consider various feeding options. Though early spring feed is normally made up of thin sugar syrup, spring feeding colonies for survival should be thick syrup or high-fructose corn syrup. See the section on various feeding techniques.

Feed Pollen Substitutes. Early spring bees must use protein sources that were stored last fall or use protein sources stored within individual bee's bodies. Pollen substitutes are available from bee supply outlets and can be fed in either dry powder form or as a patty. Home-mixed protein concoctions are also available. Due to the possibility of spreading diseases many beekeepers do not feed bee-collected pollen. Homemade mixes are not as attractive to bees, but have high protein values. Overall, commercially-produced pollen substitutes are more convenient and do not carry risks of disease contamination (See Chapter 26 for *Recipes for Pollen Supplement Mixes*).

Deal With Dead or Near-death Colonies. Initially, the beekeeper must determine the cause of death. Be certain it was not American foulbrood. If dysentery appears to have been the cause, clean fecal matter from the frames. Remove equipment back to the home apiary, clean and repair it, and get it ready for spring swarms or packages. If colonies are near death, consider combining them with other colonies. Finally, if dead colonies have honey stores remaining and are disease-free, consider giving their stores to surviving colonies.

Clean Bottom Boards. If the weather is still cold on the day manipulations are performed, do not break the cluster. However, if weather permits, break the colony down to the bottom board and scrape it clean. While there, remove entrance reducers.

Check the Queen. If possible, check the status of the queen and her brood nest. If problems exist, consider combining the colony with more prosperous colonies.

Reverse the Inner Cover. If the inner cover is reversed, as it should have been during the previous fall, this is a good time to flip it back to its warm weather position, shallow-side down.

Later Spring Management

Continue Early Spring Management Procedures. If necessary, continue early spring procedures, including feeding both sugar and pollen substitutes. Weak colonies that have survived until late spring have a better chance of becoming productive colonies. Do not be quite as quick to combine late spring weak colonies.

Examine the Brood Nest. Check the productiveness of the queen. If she is performing poorly, consider replacing her. At this time, and all other times when the brood nest is exposed, check for the presence of any disease including mites, both Varroa and tracheal. By late spring, the brood nest should be well developed and populous (probably four to six frames of developing brood).

Treat For Mites. Six to eight weeks before the spring flow begins, install Varroa mite control chemicals, preferably fluvalinate strips. Also, place grease patties in colonies to inhibit the development of tracheal mite populations. Be certain to remove all mite control compounds before the main nectar flow begins.

Reverse Hive Bodies. If the queen is not already using both hive bodies, reverse the position of hive bodies so that the brood nest is nearer the bottom board with the empty deep on top. The queen's laying tendency is to move upwardly. The empty deep on top will provide more brood nest expansion area. This procedure will help reduce swarming later in the spring and early summer.

Summer Management

Summer Nectar Flows. In most areas, after mid-summer, nectar-producing plants phase out and the annual spring/summer flow ends. As the flow ends, the beekeeper should tend to under-super. This is an attempt to force the bees to finish processing and capping honey already in the colony. Honey super removal tasks are begun and the extracting season begins. Note that many beekeepers do not remove honey until later in the fall. This is so they only need to extract once. Refer to Chapter 23, *Honey—Its Production, Processing, and Packing* for a complete discussion.

Hot Hives. Summer beekeeping activities vary with different regions. Northern areas in the USA experience cooler conditions than Southern or Southwestern areas. In any case, colonies can withstand significant amounts of heat as long as they have access to water. Slightly lifting the outer cover or staggering supers will allow for more ventilation and will help a colony deal with high heat. Note that high temperatures, in the upper 90s are normal during summer months in many parts of the United States. The occasional hot day is of little consequence to summer colonies.

Figure 33. An extremely hot hive.

Other Summer Activities. Though many colony manipulations, like requeening or making splits, can be accomplished during summer months, such activities are better left to cooler times. It is simply too hot in the bee yard for both the beekeeper and the bees to perform sophisticated hive management procedures.

CHAPTER 8

The Fall and Winter Season

The Fall Season

The Fall Honey Crop. As summer fades and temperatures begin to cool, the spring honey crop should be removed. Beekeepers who normally get a fall honey crop should begin the entire supering process again. Normally, fall honey crops are not as large as spring crops nor are they of the quality of average spring crops. Fall honey crops tend to yield darker honey with a more pronounced flavor. The same procedures used in spring supering and colony management for honey production are used for fall honey production, except that the colonies should already be at full strength.

Other Fall Management Procedures. Many other hive tasks, such as requeening or disease treatments, can be accomplished in the fall. A few beekeepers in warm climates make colony splits and winter these small colonies. During late fall, all supers should be removed and the colony prepared for the upcoming winter.

Combining Colonies

Even though colonies can be combined at nearly any time of the year, fall is the most logical time to perform the task. Occasionally, swarms that did not build up well, queenless colonies, colonies damaged by pesticides, or nucleus colonies will need to be combined with others in order for the stronger colony to pass the winter.

Figure 34. Using a sheet of newspaper to combine two colonies. The edges of the paper can be seen hanging out.

Combining Colonies Using Newspaper Sheeting. Positioning the stronger unit on the bottom board, with no outer cover on, place a single layer of newspaper over the colony. Slit the newspaper with a sharp knife two or three times to encourage bees to remove the paper. Place the weaker colony on top of the stronger unit and close the combined colony as usual. Within a day, newspaper remnants should begin appearing at the front of the colony. The two hives will combine themselves while removing the newspaper with minimal fighting. Unless one queen is preferred over the other, it is not necessary to kill one of the queens. The combined bees will decide which queen should live and which should die. The two queens may even live harmoniously for some time before one is eliminated.

Combining Colonies by Mixing the Bees from Both Colonies.

Move the weaker colony near the stronger colony. Place a wide board in front of the stronger colony. It is used as a ramp to the entrance. Remove frames as quickly as possible, shaking bees from both colonies on the ramp. It is helpful to mist the bees with thin sugar syrup while they are on the ground. Bees from both colonies will run into the hive and will ultimately eliminate one of the queens. Of course, if the smaller colony was situated in the same yard, many bees will fly back to the old location. If that is the case, move the weaker colony to a different location for a few days and then bring it back before beginning the combination procedure.

After combining colonies, wait a few days, then check the progress of the queen. If eggs are present and all seems well, the procedure went okay. If the queen cannot be found, place a frame of eggs and young brood within the middle of the combined colony. Wait a day or so, then check for queen cells. If queen cells have been started, consider purchasing a queen to requeen the colony. However, if queen cells do not show, one of the queens should be okay. Combination procedures can be performed late in the year, if a warm day comes along. If the weather is too cold, both units will stay clustered and will not combine into one colony.

Figure 35. A wintering honey bee cluster.

The Winter Season

Cluster Dynamics. In anticipation of the up-coming winter season, it is the beekeeper's management goal to assist, as much as possible, in getting the colony prepared for winter. Though honey bee wintering biology is a surprisingly complicated system of temperature and humidity regulatory procedures, the basic procedure is nothing more than a group of cold-blooded animals (bees) huddling together to pool their warmth (clustering). The wintering honey bee cluster works actively to control its environment when the ambient temperature is lower than they can tolerate as individual bees. Single bees have limited capacity to respond to low temperatures. The become increasingly unable to function, as individuals, at about 50° F. Single bees will soon die if held at more than a few hours at temperatures much lower than 45°–50° F. The honey bee relies on sugar as its source of energy. As the temperature drops, sugar absorption in the bee's gut is increasingly restricted. Ultimately, the chilled bee dies of starvation.

The winter cluster generates heat by the micro-vibrations or flexing of individual bee's flight muscles. These movements are so small as to be invisible to humans. Beekeepers frequently think that bees have a special attribute when it comes to heat generation, but in fact, many insects can generate heat as readily as honey bees. The honey bee's talent is in controlling heat production over long periods. So long as they are well fed, developing honey bee larvae are also excellent producers of cluster heat. The clustering behavior of adult bees and developing bees fundamentally makes the bee colony become a larger animal rather than a collection of many smaller ones.

The cluster of bees in an average colony forms a generalized spherical shape. As a colony is cooled, clustering becomes evident at about 56° F. There may still be small satellite clusters near the main cluster. At about 32° F, all bees should be in the main cluster. The temperature of the edge of the outer cluster is maintained at about 55° F while the brood nest in the center of the cluster is maintained at about 95° F. As the ambient temperature drops, a cluster has two ways to maintain its temperature: (1) cluster contraction and (2) increased heat generation. Contracting the cluster results in decreased surface area and increases the insulation capabilities of the outer shell of bees. To maintain controlled temperatures, the cluster expands or contracts depending on environmental temperatures. As falling temperatures drop below 41° F, cluster compaction is at its maximum. Increasingly, bees within the interior of the cluster must generate more heat by flexing their flight muscles to generate heat. Healthy colonies with good supplies of honey have withstood temperatures as low as -40° F for extended periods.

Food Stores. Established recommendations are for 90–100 pounds of honey, or ripened sugar syrup, for strong colony survival from October to April in the northern tier of the United States and parts of Canada. Smaller colonies can survive on smaller honey stores (about 27 pounds), but will expend more energy on heat production and will build up much more slowly in the spring than stronger colonies. Generally, a three-deep colony, with a telescoping outer cover, should have a gross weight of 175 pounds in October.

Strong wintering colonies can exist on surprisingly small quantities of honey—about 3–4 pounds per month until brood rearing starts. Upon which, honey consumption increases dramatically. Occasionally, strong colonies that wintered well die in early spring. This is due to depletion caused by increased larval food and warmth demands. Honey in the comb is the best winter feed for a colony although colonies pass winter seasons using well-ripened sugar syrup as food. Since they can take more cleansing flights, bees in colonies located in warmer climates can frequently survive on sugar syrup alone. If extra food must be supplied, the feed should be given early enough for the bees to process and store in combs. (See Chapter 9, *Supplemental Sugar Feeding—Helping a Hungry Colony*). The tendency for the wintering cluster is to move upwardly. Food stores should be on the sides of the cluster in the bottom deep and directly above the cluster in upper deeps. After brood rearing is initiated in late winter and early spring, the cluster is forced to stay in a fixed position—usually within upper deeps. Warm weather spells are necessary for bees to relocate stores from surrounding frames closer to the brood nest.

Having high quality stores readily available and properly positioned, not only insure more successful wintering, but will assist in lowering incidence of diseases. Nosema is probably the most serious brood disease of the wintering colony. (See Chapter 27, *Recognizing and Treating the Bee Hive for Common Diseases and Pests*). An infected colony, at best, results in a weakened colony and, at worst, results in the colony's death. Naturally, standard mite treatments should be practiced as recommended.

Internal Colony Moisture. Internal colony moisture places stress on wintering hives that may facilitate the onset of diseases such as Nosema. For every 10 pounds of honey that a colony consumes, about one gallon of water is produced. Colonies should be ventilated to allow the escape of moisture-laden air.

A common ventilation procedure is drilling a single 3/4" auger hole just below the hand hold on one end of the brood chamber. Depending on the climate, both ends may be drilled. While many beekeepers prefer this procedure, it will require additional work to close entrances when the colony is relocated in the future. A second common procedure is to raise one end of the inner cover approximately 1/4" with stones, wooden spacers, or twigs and replace the outer cover. If flat board covers, also called "migratory

Figure 36. An acceptable amount of frost in the wintering hive. Some frost is not harmful, but not too much.

covers," are used, raise them the same as inner covers. Such upper openings allow escape of air and allow bees a higher entrance should the lower entrance become blocked with dead bees, ice, snow, or leaves. Internal frost is an indicator of ventilation adequacy. Some light frost within the colony is appropriate, but excessive frost and ice is unacceptable. During warm periods, ice that is inside the hive melts and cold water drips on the cluster. However, in cold climates, the opposite extreme is equally harmful. Excessive ventilation would result in wider temperature fluctuations with increased cluster temperatures and food consumption.

Winter Management Manipulations.

Inner Covers. As a management procedure, inner covers should be turned over to have the deep side down during winter months. The extra space beneath the inner cover will give the bees more space to cluster and to move food stores to different locations. However, the inner cover should promptly be returned to its normal position before the nectar flow begins or there is risk of burr comb being put in the extra space.

Entrance Reduction. Even if lower entrances will be blocked by ice or snow, they should still be reduced. Hive entrance dimensions vary; generally, the entrance height should not exceed 3/8" in height. This height will restrict mice and other small animals from entering. Commonly, standard entrance reducers restrict the entrance to 3/8" x 1".

Hive Stands. Colonies winter better if placed on hive stands that are at least four inches off the ground. Types of hive stands have been discussed in Chapter 2, *The Beekeeper's Equipment.*

Figure 37. A hive with a wooden entrance-reducing cleat.

Sunlight. Ideally, colonies should receive morning sunlight, regardless of the climate. In hot climates, afternoon shade may be helpful to reduce heat. Beekeepers differ on which direction to face the colony. Some recommend facing colonies toward the south in order to avoid cold north winter winds. Others say to face to the east in order to get the first rays of the morning sun. It probably does not matter.

Windbreaks. In cold climates, windbreaks can be useful in helping colonies control internal hive temperatures. Breaks can be tree lines, fences, hills, buildings, boulders, or other ground vegetation.

Frost Pockets. Occasionally, frost pockets are problems for hives. Avoid placing a yard in a low-lying location where cold air sinks and coldness is held even during warmer parts of the day.

Winter Management from the Past. In the past, considerable time and research was directed toward wrapping colonies in various insulated materials such as corrugated board or tarpaper. Additionally, colonies have been relocated to special cellars. Even designated buildings and electric hive heaters have been constructed for wintering bee colonies. These advanced wintering procedures are necessary only in the coldest of climates and will not be needed by most USA beekeepers. One of the common complaints with insulating hives is that hive insulation will keep coldness in on the occasional warm winter day thereby preventing bees from taking winter cleansing flights. Even so, future recommendations will include some type of hive insulation for temperature regulation.

Key Points for Over-Wintering Honey Bee Colonies
1. Adequate honey and pollen stores in the proper location (90–100 pounds of honey in October).
2. Large, healthy population of adult bees. Smaller colonies should be combined and splits made next spring.
3. Wind protection.
4. Disease and mite control.
5. Upper entrances for ventilation and winter exits.
6. Bottom entrance reductions to restrict mice.
7. Winter inspections. Do not break winter clusters, but reposition or provide honey stores as necessary.
8. Hive stands.

Inspecting Hives in Late Winter. In reality, only dead hives (or hives that will die anyway) can be inspected on a cold winter day. Nevertheless, there are some ways that will help a hive prepare for spring if the hive is worked during one of those rare warm days during winter months.

During mid to late March, around mid-morning on a warm and sunny day hives may be worked safely if done quickly. Before opening the hive, have a look around it first. What is the story at the hive entrance? Are there lots of dead bees, a few dead bees or no dead bees at all? Surprisingly, no dead bees out front usually predict a colony that is already dead. A few dead bees are normal while approximately two thousand are probably too many. Be suspicious of some kind of disease or pest inside the hive. Any skunk odors or animal droppings around the hive? Animals constantly annoying a wintering colony can cause serious disturbances to that hive.

Now smoke the hive and remove the cover. Where are the bees in the colony? They are probably going to be at the top right under the inner cover. Break down the hive to the bottom board, but leave the bee cluster unbroken in its deep hive box. Is there anything interesting on the bottom board? Is there any mouse damage? If so, use entrance reducers next fall. Using the hive tool, scrape (or replace) the bottom board. Now put the deep hive body that has the bee cluster back on the bottom board so the bee nest is now on the bottom board. How heavy is the hive? As discussed earlier, most colonies starve in early spring (not during the cold winter) after brood production has begun. If it is lightweight, feed them within the next few days. Feed them heavy sugar syrup—not thin syrup.

Now, gently pull a side frame out but not from the center. This risks injuring the queen. Within the extra space of the removed frame, take out a second frame toward the center. What does the brood pattern look like? Is it a nice solid frame of brood or a smelly spotty frame? If there is a bee disease problem, get help. Some bee diseases are contagious and persistent (American foulbrood). If there is no brood at all, check for the presence of eggs. Upon finding no eggs or no queen, consider combining the colony with another. This will increase the strength of the second hive, allowing it to build up quicker. In the spring, buy a queen and make a split so there will be two colonies by the spring nectar flow. Put the frames back in the same position. Put the empty deep equipment on top of the colony and close the hive. Do not keep the colony open any longer than necessary. It probably would not hurt if the entrance reducer were left out now. An entrance reducer keeps out mice—not coldness, but leaving it in for another month will not hurt either. It is important to reverse the position of the deeps.

Concerning this specific hypothetical colony, the beekeeper now:

1. Has an idea of how well it is wintering,
2. Has cleaned the bottom board and reversed hive bodies so the bees are near the bottom board (this inhibits swarming later on),
3. Has an idea of the health of the brood and the quantity of honey stores and
4. Has extra space above the brood nest—all ready for nest expansion and nectar storage as the spring season progresses.

The Winter-Killed Colony

The appearance of a winter-killed colony is obvious. The bees are found dead, in a tight ball nearly anywhere within the colony. Many bees will have their heads, or even their complete bodies, stuck into cells. Though there may be some honey fragments scattered within the hive, the

Figure 38. A winter-killed colony.

amount of honey stores is small. Alternatively, there may be abundant honey, but it is located away from the cluster.

If the winter-killed colony did not die from a disease like American foulbrood, as many bees as possible should be dumped out as much as possible. Many times, the dead bees within cells can be jarred loose from the colony by rapping the frame sharply, comb side down, on the edge of the hive. Again, assuming no disease is present, the equipment can readily be used again next spring as a new home for a swarm or a package.

CHAPTER 9

Supplemental Sugar Feeding—
Helping a Hungry Colony

Supplemental feeding is a common way to get the bees started off to a good productive year. Fall feeding can be important also, but the feeding procedure must be started long before cold weather arrives. It is much easier to feed colonies during warm months, rather than during the erratic, cool days of the following spring.

Getting Bees to Take the Feed. Bees have no obvious way to transmit information concerning food that is literally in front of their nose. Frequently, a colony that has just had a feeder installed will show a great deal of flight activity near the front of the hive. Individual bees, having discovered the feeder, have no easy way to tell other bees of the find. In their dance, they essentially say that a food source is somewhere within a few yards of the hive when in reality, it is probably somewhere within the hive. Each bee that takes syrup from a feeder must learn to do it individually. Some bees learn faster than others. Indeed, some bees will never learn to take the food efficiently. This inability of some colonies to learn to take syrup explains why some colonies take syrup so fast while others consume the syrup so slowly that it may actually have time to ferment.

If there are only a few colonies to be fed, frames of honey (sugar syrup) can be taken from "smart" colonies and given to the slower colonies. This is labor intensive, but it will get food in the right form and quantity to all colonies. Intensive feeding will, on occasion, stimulate brood rearing. It is probably best to have a colony too strong going into winter as opposed to being weak. Having them produce brood is the lesser of the potential evils.

How Much Feed Is Enough? Though a simple question, the answer is difficult. Directly answered, feed enough sugar to meet the colony's needs. Feeding a colony for winter food stores will require much more food than feeding a colony for spring stimulation. Generally, when natural food sources become available, the colony will abandon the artificial food source and move to the natural sources. Essentially, the colony will tell you when it has enough.

When To Stop Feeding? A strong colony going into winter will need around fifteen deep frames of capped honey. There are many variables not the least of which will be the climate where the colony is wintering. However, even colonies in warm climates will require similar amounts of food stores. The biggest difference is that colonies in warmer climates will be able to take more cleansing flights. This will enable warm-climate bees to winter easier on lower quality food stores. However, taking more flights during times when absolutely no nectar is available only deletes honey stores more rapidly.

A two-story colony going into winter should have a gross weight of (at least) 165–185 pounds. Again this depends on many variables. For the average person, the colony should feel so heavy as to be difficult to tilt from behind. If the colony is obviously light and can be shifted easily, continue to feed it. As the weather becomes cold, bees will finally stop taking the feed.

When feeding for food storage rather than stimulation, feed thick syrup. Two common sugar syrups are high fructose corn syrup, which can be fed directly from the container and sugar syrup that should be made from hot water and granulated sugar. Keep in mind that five pounds of sugar in 50 gallons of water is still just five pounds of sugar, so the thicker the syrup, the greater the benefit to the colony. Since it requires no mixing, high fructose corn syrup that is purchased from bee supply companies is easier to feed, but it may be difficult to get in small quantities.

What Kind Of Feeder Should Be Used? Through the years, beekeepers have devised an incredible number of ways to get sugar to bee colonies. Many of these feeders have restrictions such as weather conditions, hive size, cost, or quantity of syrup delivered. Feeders range dramatically in complexity ranging from granulated sugar poured on the top bars to gasoline-driven comb filler.

Open Feeding

Open feeding is one of the simplest ways to get syrup to a large number of colonies. The problem is that the bees may not always be from the colonies of the beekeeper providing the food. In addition, weaker colonies may have problems getting their fair share when competing with stronger colonies. Until mites destroyed much of the feral honey bee populations in the United States, open feeding was not commonly used. It may be time to try it again.

Essentially, all that is required is a large container such as a galvanized tub, a 55-gallon drum cut

Figure 39. Open feeding peppermint-scented sugar syrup from a 55-gallon drum.

in half, or a plastic child's wading pool; put sugar syrup in it along with either gravel or straw placed in it for the bees to stand on while feeding. Keeping it loosely covered will help keep out rain. Do not put so much sugar syrup out that the bees cannot take it in a day or so. Colonies have been known to take 60 gallons of syrup in one day. Naturally, be cautious when doing this in crowded neighborhoods. Do not try it in cold weather. It may take a few hours for foraging bees to find the food. Once they do, it is a fast way to get stores to the colonies. As always, spreading disease is a serious concern with feeding syrup in this fashion.

External Feeders

External feeders are accessible from the outside of the hive and are easily accessible without opening the hive. External feeders are usually beekeeper designs, except for the Boardman feeder that is a familiar feeder to most beekeepers.

Boardman Feeders. Being little more than an inverted canning jar capped with a perforated lid and fitted to a hollow base, the Boardman feeder is practical and simple. It slips into the colony entrance and is readily accessible to the bees. It is easy to tell when it needs filled. Additionally, it is easy to fill without disturbing the bees, it is easy to install it, plus it is inexpensive. This feeder sounds perfect, but it has problems. It can incite robbing if it leaks near the entrance of the hive. It requires glass jars, which easily break in route to the bee yard and most importantly, bees cannot readily use this feeder during cool weather.

Figure 40. A single story hive with a Boardman feeder in use.

Internal Feeders

Division Board Feeders. In beekeeping years long ago, there were pieces of beekeeping equipment named division boards, also referred to as follower boards that were used to compartmentalize a hive. Essentially, four or five frames were partitioned off using a temporary wall made of a one-half-inch board. It was only a small step to make the board wider and hollow to use as a container for an internal hive feeder. Earlier ones were made from wood, but modern ones are plastic. They take the place of a single frame and are usually located at the sides of the brood nest. To fill it, maneuver hive equipment so the filler opening is reachable. Fill it with about a gallon of sugar syrup. It needs to have a float in the feeder or bees will drown. The bees readily take feed from this gadget. It requires removing a frame and moving equipment to fill it.

Hive Top Feeders. There are many models of hive top feeders— including several antique models. As with division board feeders, current hive top feeders are now made of plastic. The basic premise of all styles of hive top feeders is for bees to move through openings up into the feeder that is positioned directly beneath the inner cover. The positioning of the various openings varies with the style of feeder. They are easy to fill and have a large capacity, sometimes as much as two gallons. However, they must be completely removed before any other hive manipulation can be accomplished. Older style feeders had a tendency to seep, rather than outright leak. Naturally, this would encourage robbing.

Friction-Top Feeders. Simple, efficient feeders can be devised by using friction-top metal cans with a few small holes punched into the lid. The can is then inverted over the handhold in the inner cover. Bees can move into the small area between the inner cover and the lid of the pail, then feed from syrup drops hanging there. Since a vacuum forms in the can

Figure 41. An assortment of various hive feeders. (A bucket feeder, two top feeders, a division board feeder, and a Boardman feeder.)

that prevents syrup from flowing out too fast, it is important that the lid fit tightly. There are also friction-top plastic pails that are in use now. Though not necessary, the pail can be surrounded by an empty deep super. This will keep the feeder from being knocked off by wind or animals.

Comb Fillers

Gasoline-Powered Fillers. Comb fillers are used for spraying syrup into cells. In this manner, entire frames, full of syrup, can be placed near the brood nest. Bees will consolidate and manipulate the syrup into honey or will use it immediately. This is probably the fastest way for bees to get sugar syrup feed. However, sugar syrup that is not consolidated will granulate quickly. This is not really a major problem for the bees, but it does result in sticky, crystallized syrup all over.

Figure 42. A gasoline-powered comb filler.

Garden Type Compression Sprayers. Common "pump-up" garden sprayers can be used in exactly the same manner as described in the section above. They are much cheaper, but will only fill a few frames before the sprayer, itself, must be refilled.

Dry Feed

Candy Boards. Candy boards are not being used much any more, probably because they are labor intensive. A fondant-type candy was made from simple recipes, molded into a wooden frame and put on top of the colony. A recipe to make sugar candy is:

Sugar Candy Recipe for Feeding Bees
1. 15 pounds of sugar
2. 3 pounds of glucose or white syrup
3. 4 cups of water
4. ½ teaspoon of cream of tartar

Dissolve sugar in water by stirring and boiling the mixture until the temperature of the syrup is at 242° F. Let it cool to 180° F and beat thick. Pour the mixture into molds and allow it to harden.

Feeding Dry Sugar. This is the simplest, cheapest, and probably least effective way to feed bees. Normally, granulated sugar is piled around the inner cover handhold. Bees will need water to covert dry sugar to simple syrup. Occasionally, some bees will laboriously remove the sugar and toss it out front, but most hives will use it reasonably well. This procedure is frequently used during hard cold weather, but will also work during late fall to early spring.

Granulated Corn Syrup. Corn syrup granulates easily. Some beekeepers will take (literally) handfuls of granulated high fructose corn syrup and spread it on the top bars of the brood nest. Messy as it is, it is also fast, simple, and near the bees. It works well if the sticky hands can be tolerated.

Types of Sugar to Feed Bees

Occasionally, sugar can be acquired from some unusual "free" sugar sources. Contaminated soft drink syrup, out-of-date Jell-O® products, and by-products from chewing gum manufacture are examples. If a junk sugar source sounds too good to be true, it probably is. Any sugar product that has many indigestible by-products will cause the bees harm during winter months. This includes bulk powdered sugar which has small amounts of corn starch in it.

If corn syrup is to be used, use only high fructose corn syrup. It is best to get syrup from a bee supply dealer. Beekeepers normally prefer corn syrup with about 42% solids. Granulated sugar can be purchased in bulk from wholesale grocer outlets.

Feeding Bees in Cool Weather

Feeding bees in cool weather is never a good plan, but sometimes it cannot be avoided. Select a feeder that can be filled without undue disruption to the colony and get the feed as close to the bees as possible in a form that is as ready to use as possible. Feeding bees in hard winter is nearly impossible. If wintering bees must be fed, combs of capped honey are excellent food sources, but are not normally available. Use dry sugar on the inner cover. Unfortunately, the chances for getting a strong colony coming out of winter are not good.

CHAPTER 10

Locations of Bee Yards

Beekeepers have shown great creativity through the years when setting up hive locations. A site where beehives are located is called either the apiary or bee yard. If the yard is not located at home, the location is called an outyard. There are many common attributes that all bee locations should have although some of these characteristics are more important than others.

Figure 43. A good location for a bee yard.

Characteristics That Locations Must Have

Permission from the Landowner. Obviously, if the land does not belong to the beekeeper, permission must be obtained before putting bees on it. Positioning bees on another's property has occasionally occurred when bee colonies were temporarily set out for pollination purposes. For established yards, it would be a good idea if the land-owner would sign an agreement indicating where the colonies are, how many exist, and who the rightful owner is. Occasionally, landowners have died leaving all their possessions in probate until all property was dispersed.

Locations That Are Readily Accessible. A beekeeper must be able to get to the yard when the colonies need working. Locked gates, muddy paths, maturing field crops, and re-directed access lanes can all be hindrances to getting to the bees. Many times, hives are moved at night. Such hindrances are magnified then. The location should be well drained. Accepting locations that are flooded part of the year will not be conducive to good hive management.

Water, Nectar, and Pollen Sources. Bees need water year-round, but they especially need water during hot months. The farther away the water source the more energy they will have to expend to get it. Nectar and pollen are normally available in most locations in the USA. However, some locations are obviously better than others.

Reasonable Safety from Pesticide Exposure. There are not many places left where foraging bees are not at risk to pesticide exposure. Near sweet corn fields and cotton fields are locations where bees are killed in significant numbers. Sometimes, such locations are convenient and may be justified on that count. Otherwise, after a yard is set up, watch for pesticide kills for the first year or so. If many more than a few thousand bees are killed at one time, consider re-locating the yard.

Desirable (but unnecessary) Characteristics of Apiary Locations

Windbreaks. Windbreaks are a requirement in some cold weather locations, but most locations do not require them. Windbreaks are frequently more important for beekeepers comfort when working bees.

Morning Sun and Afternoon Shade. These are desirable attributes, but colonies survive without them. However, colonies located in deep shade in cool climates may not prosper as well as those in sunlight. Unable to take advantage of foraging possibilities, they stay cool too long during daylight hours .

Frost Pockets. Avoid low-lying areas at the base of hillsides that capture and hold cold air, thereby keeping colonies cool throughout the day.

Storage Facility. A storage building in or near the bee yard is a luxury, but is not required. It just means more work and more forgotten items if everything must be transported to the yard each trip.

Scenic Vistas. Most beekeepers work bees because it is enjoyable. Having a nice view while working bees is particularly pleasant, but again, it is not a requirement.

Being a Good Neighbor. In reality, beehives can be kept nearly anywhere. However, keeping neighbors happy is always a necessity. Do not force bee colonies on someone else. If possible, place fencing or hedges around hives to make bees fly higher. Keep dependable water sources available in order to discourage bees from foraging at the neighbor's pool or birdbath. Finally, try to control swarming.

CHAPTER 11

Moving Bee Colonies

Reasons for Moving Bee Colonies

Probably 50% of all bee colonies within the United States are moved at least once each year. Beekeepers may need to move a few colonies. In other cases, thousands of hives may require relocating. While moving beehives is common, it can certainly still be eventful. Successfully moving bee hives will require careful planning, dependable equipment, and some good luck.

Purchasing Colonies. When colonies are purchased from another beekeeper, invariably the hives will need to be moved to a new location. Potentially a good deal of work, with preparation, most bee colony moves go smoothly.

Commercial Pollination. Commercial honey bee pollination can be relocating just one colony to a grower's planting or, depending on grower needs, it can be moving several thousand to a grower's planting. Either way, colonies are moved for supplemental pollination.

Problem Yards. Everything changes eventually. For example, a car dealership moves next to a long-established bee yard or a farmer changes crops or puts cattle in the area. Possibly, new homes are built too close by. Pesticide use increases and bee kills become excessive. Frequently, good yards become problem yards thereby requiring relocation.

When To Move. There are two obvious times to move colonies, during the day or evening hours. If the move is long enough, it may actually require both day and evening hours. The advantages to a day move are that one can see what is being done and where one is going. However, so can the bees. The advantage to an evening move is that all the bees are in the hive and no stragglers are abandoned in the old yard. Beekeepers moving considerable numbers of colonies may elect to leave a few trap colonies behind when moving bees during the day. All foraging bees returning to the yard will find that they have only a few colonies to choose from and will eventually drift to the trap colonies. Later, the beekeeper can return with a smaller truck and retrieve the few remaining colonies, however, this procedure will require two trips.

A Short Move with a Few Colonies

Staples. Hive staples, available from bee supply companies, are frequently used to prepare a hive for transport. These staples are effective and simple to use. However, hammer pounding disturbs the bees and staples must be removed from the colony or they will snag on. Additionally, after several years of colony moves, the sites where the staples are attached will become damaged.

When using staples, angle the staples so the colony will not slip on the bottom board. There is no effective way to staple a telescoping outer cover to the colony. They should be removed for transport.

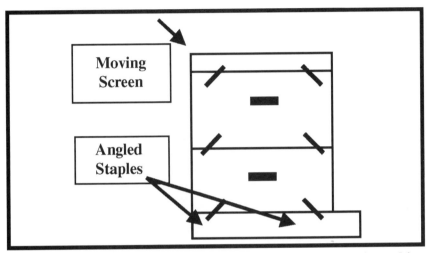

Figure 44. Correct angle for inserting staples when securing a hive for transportation.

Figure 45. A nylon-ratchet-strapped hive ready for a move.

Straps. Ratchet straps are available at any hardware or building supply company. These straps are excellent for securing a hive for transport and will also secure the outer cover in the process. The disadvantages are that the hive must be lifted, in order to get the straps underneath. Occasionally, straps can be torn or cut as the colony is slid onto the truck. Regardless, these straps generally work well.

Battens. Small battens or boards can be tacked to the sides of a colony and provide the same services as staples.

They, too, will require pounding on the hive and will require removal once the trip has ended. Lathing for batten strips can be purchased at building supply companies or can be ripped from larger boards. In addition to putting them on the sides, placing one on the back and front will prevent the hive from slipping on the bottom board as was discussed in the section on staple use.

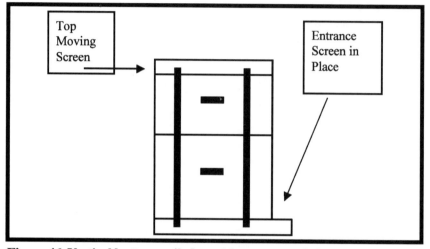

Figure 46. Vertical battens nailed to a hive to secure it for transportation.

Transportation Screens. For most hobby beekeepers, when moving colonies, both the top and the entrance should be closed with screen or some other closing device. Bees can quickly suffocate within the hive. Although it is rare to have hives to freeze while in transit, it is possible to have hives die from heat and suffocation. Therefore, it would be better to provide too much ventilation rather than too little.

Aluminum Screen is Commonly Used to Improvise an Entrance Closing Device. Use a piece of screen three inches wide and a couple of inches longer than the entrance. Bend the ends of the screen until it is the exact length of the entrance. Then, gently push the screen into the hive entrance. The screen will form a v-shape and the tension of the screen will hold it in place. Plastic screen (or vinyl) is not strong enough to support the weight of bees piling against it while in the v-shape. Bees will begin to escape as the vinyl screen sags.

Many types of entrance closing ideas are currently in use. A strip of 8-mesh hardware cloth cut to approximately 3" by the length of the entrance makes a quick, effective closing device. The entrance closer[3] is adjustable and simple to install.

---

[3]Manufactured by Miller and Sons, Dundee, Ohio 44624

Figure 47. A commercially manufactured entrance closing device.[3]

Figure 48. A colony with a top and front screen in preparation for moving.

Top Screens. In addition, top screens should be used for long trips or during warm weather. An effective top screen device can be made from a wood rim, the same size as the brood chamber and about 3" deep. Hardware (8-mesh) cloth can be tacked to the top of the rim. Finally, the rim is attached, in some way, to the top of the hive.

Hand Trucks and Hydraulic Tailgates. Any mechanical device that assists the movement and loading of hives will be relief to the bee-keeper moving multiple colonies. Hand trucks are useful in getting the hive to the truck and can even be used to roll colonies onto low trailers to be towed behind another vehicle. Hydraulic tailgates are an obvious luxury and are perfect for loading hives onto trucks.

After having described many of the various options open to beekeepers who are planning to move bee hives, there are occasions when colonies are just picked up and moved with little to no preparation. This is always risky. Many times, hives that have not been opened in a while are propolized together and will withstand the move without incident. Such trips should be short and after dark when all the bees will stay within the colony. Again, this procedure is not a good one and, if possible, should not be used.

Equipment for a Commercial Move

Sideline or commercial beekeepers who move colonies routinely have specialized equipment designed specifically for this purpose. Hive Loaders mounted on trucks, mechanized hand trucks and skid-steer loaders for loading palletized colonies are types of equipment common to the migratory beekeeper. Rather than restrict individual colonies, the entire load is covered with a giant plastic net. Such nets are heavy, expensive and must be kept in good repair.

Figure 49. A commercial load of beehives. Hives are on the front and supers are on the back. Note the netting covering the hives up front.

Potential Problems

Though a carefully planned trip usually carries the day, occasionally problems arise. Stopping for fuel with a few bees escaping from hives can cause concern among the other customers who are also using the fueling station. Naturally, there can be mechanical breakdowns or worse, the occasional accident. Be certain to take along a smoker and protective gear. During warm months, include a water hose for hosing down hot colonies in case the load begins to overheat. Having a chain or towing strap is not a bad idea either. Though conditions may be fine at the original site, it is possible to find the new yards to be wet and boggy. It is always a good idea to have another beekeeper ride along to help with the procedure, but this is not always possible and maybe not even be necessary if the load is small enough.

CHAPTER 12

Robbing Behavior of Honey Bees

What is Robbing Behavior?

When colonies are near each other in the bee yard, occasionally a behavior manifests itself that beekeepers call "robbing". In times of a nectar dearth, forager bees will forage on neighboring hives' honey resources. That is all that is taken, no pollen, no wax, no propolis, and no brood—only honey. The behavior can become intense with bees trying to get into any crack or opening in the victimized colony.

Figure 50. Bees robbing supers.

The event usually occurs during summer months, when colony populations are high and there is no nectar flow. It can start reasonably slow, but build to a level approaching being completely out of control in only a few minutes. Normally, weak colonies are attacked, but sometimes powerful colonies can be under siege also. Though the exact reasons are unclear, robbing may not be a completely natural behavior. In nature, there would rarely be ten, fifteen, or even more colonies so close together in one location. With so many unemployed foragers available, great numbers of foragers can be directed to the colony being attacked. In most cases, the beekeeper is responsible for either. She or he has opened a colony and has performed some assigned beekeeping procedure thereby leaving the open colony vulnerable. Opening all colonies at once may put the colonies on alert, thereby reducing the robbing tendencies.

No doubt, robbing occurs in the wild, but is rare. A colony's tree is blown down or a colony dies of mite predation and honey resources are left unprotected, so neighboring robber bees move in and clean out the residue. However, these are occasional events.

How to Control Robbing

The colony or colonies being robbed should have all extraneous openings closed. The entrance should nearly close allowing only one or two bees to enter or exit at once. Under desperate conditions, beekeepers use wads of grass to stuff into every entrance. Pick up all burr combs and cover supers or better yet, get them out of the yard. Close up the colony under attack and let things settle down. Does all this infer beehives cannot be worked during the summer? No, but a beekeeper may not necessarily be able to manipulate a colony in late August the same way that it would have been manipulated during the spring flow. If the danger of robbing is present, open the colony in question, perform the necessary tasks and get out as quickly as possible. Keep smoking all the colonies and shut down the entrances to the colony that was just manipulated. Keep the yard free of other attractive sources such as empty supers or comb scrapings. Robbers can be diverted to honey sources that have been left out to be intentionally robbed. For instance, if extensive beehive manipulations are planned for late summer, an attractive pile of comb cappings or some other food source can be placed in the yard. Give the bees a day or so to find the food source, thereby keeping them occupied. Robbing episodes are excellent opportunities for diseases to be spread. Do not use contaminated combs or honey of unknown origin.

Bee Blowers can be instrumental in initiating robbing activities. The aroma of fresh honey and comb is blown across the yard making it even easier for robber foragers to find the open colonies. However, this process is usually self-limiting in that all colonies are ultimately opened and supers removed. Once a colony is challenged, it will divert robbing behavior to colony defense and mitigate robbing activities.

In many instances, small colonies such as queen mating nuclei are in danger of robbing. In such cases, robbing screens can be installed. These devices require bees to learn to use specific routes when entering and leaving the colony. Impatient robbers will fly directly to the entrance where they will be stopped from entering while trained bees are able to use the known entrances. Along the same lines, a robber cage is useful under specified conditions. It is simply a screen cage, usually measuring about four feet square and about five feet tall having neither top nor bottom. The robbing cage, with the beekeeper and the hive inside, is set over the colony to be manipulated. Bees leaving the colony will find the open top and leave. The cage confuses robbers that are attempting to fly directly into the colony entrance. Once the management tasks are finished, the entrance is reduced, so small that only a bee or two can enter at once. Using this cage, the open colony is never directly exposed to the ravages of robber bees.

Figure 51. A collapsible robbing cage with an access door.

Be aware that the practice of allowing bees to rob extracted supers from which honey has been extracted as a "treat" may encourage bees to rob other colonies. This process of open robbing is not recommended because the beekeeper runs the risk of losing control in the bee yard. A better procedure would be to place the empty, wet supers on colonies and let bees clean the honey residue from the inside. Many times, such wet supers are also wet on the outside and will attract robbers to the hive having the supers stacked on.

Robber Bee Behavior

Robber bees have an irregular, flighty behavior. They will hover around the colony entrance or try to fly directly into the hive. In a strong colony guard bees attack robbers. Both bees will roll around in combat. If not killed, robbers will lose much of their body hair during such skirmishes and will take on a glossy black look. In the true sense of the word, these robbers are not villains, but are aggressive foragers out to get food for their colony anywhere they can.

Progressive Robbing

If robbers are successful at getting into a colony and proffering a load of honey, they begin to acquire the odor of the victimized colony. Finally, they carry the odor of both colonies and can freely enter either colony. Such robbing behavior is called "progressive robbing" and is much more difficult to determine or control. No doubt progressive robbing goes on to some degree all summer, but all things being equal, the honey that a colony's progressive robbers steals from another colony is ultimately stolen by progressive robbers from other colonies.

CHAPTER 13

Bees in the Garden

People frequently want to keep bees to accent either a flower or vegetable garden or for pollination. For such people, honey production is reduced in importance and pollination is placed in the forefront of the beekeeping effort. Large, populous hives are not always desirable. Keeping bees within a garden setting is a specialized form of beekeeping instigated by the recent decline in all bee populations, including honey bees. In fact, all bees, not just honey bees, should be encouraged in the garden setting.

Figure 52. An aerial view of part of The Ohio State University bee plant garden (Wooster, Ohio).

Many insect species are common visitors to the flower and vegetable gardens. While a few insects are undesirable pests, many are beneficial pollinators. Butterflies and moths are pretty pollinators and add a colorful component to the diversified garden environment. However, bees are pollination workhorses. Within the USA, there are several thousand species of both native and exotic bees that quietly go about their pollination chores within the gardens, orchards, and fields.

Bumble Bees. Bumble bees (*Bombus* sp.) are the teddy bears of the garden. They are native to the United States and diverse in both color and function. While it is possible to offer artificial domiciles to bumbles under specific conditions, nearly all bumble bees are wild and will find their own nest sites. They will select such places as old mice nests, underground cavities, or hollows in basement walls. Unfortunately, there is no way to predict where a queen bumble bee will choose for a home cite. Bumble bees construct annual nests and live for only one season. The large bumble bees that are common visitors on early spring flowers are queens that are essentially working mothers, spending part of their day foraging and part of the day nurturing a few cells of incubating brood. As the family grows, so does the efficiency of the nest. During July and August, young male and female bumble bees are produced. Newly-mated queens find a protected location in which to pass the winter in anticipation of next year's season. Bumble bees produce only enough honey for their own use. Consequently, they have no value as honey producers. These large-bodied pollination generalists are excellent pollinators. Select insecticides and insect control techniques that are sensitive to the needs and survival of bumble bee pollinators.

Native Bees. There are innumerable native bees that are small and unobtrusive in their pollination functions. Some live in small holes in wood while others nest in cavities in the ground. Specialized techniques are available for large growers providing artificial domiciles for bees such as leafcutters or alkali bees.

Figure 53. A nesting box for native bee pollinators.

However, these procedures are essentially beyond the scope of most backyard gardeners. A recommendation is to leave as large an undisturbed area as possible somewhere on the property for native bees to nest. Naturally, some gardens will have greater native bee populations than others and some years will be better than others. Frequently, leafcutter bees (*Osmia* sp.) can be attracted to hardwood blocks having numerous holes that are 1/4" to 5/16" wide and approximately four inches deep. Untreated wood can be purchased at building supply outlets or pieces of firewood can be squared and used. Blocks should be replaced every couple of years. Again, some locations and blocks are more attractive than others. There are no guarantees.

Honey Bees. The common honey bee (*Apis mellifera L.*) is a generalist and is not native to the USA. Honey bees are good pollinators, but are not always the best. The major difference between the honey bee and other bees already discussed is that the honey bee nest is essentially perennial and commonly produces a honey surplus. Another feature of honey bee husbandry is that they readily accept artificial domiciles (hives).

Honey bees, as do all other bees, have a documented disease and pest complex (See Chapter 27, *Recognizing and Treating the Beehive for Common Diseases and Pests*). Recently, the establishment of two new predacious mites—tracheal mites and Varroa mites, has ravaged honey bees. Although there are adequate control methods for these pests within managed colonies, wild honey bee colonies have been hit very hard. The immediate recovery of the wild honey bee is not assured. Increasingly, gardeners have shown an interest in maintaining honey bee hives for pollination, honey production and environmental contributions.

Beekeeping Gardeners

In many ways, gardeners are not traditional beekeepers. Beekeepers usually desire large pollination potentials and honey crops, whereas gardeners frequently desire smaller colonies that are more compatible with a diversified garden. Bee breeders have spent more than 150 years selecting for honey bees that produce large populations of bees, large honey crops, and large pollination outputs. A mature honey bee hive, during summer months, could have as many as 60,000 bees and weigh upwards to 300 pounds. Most gardeners simply do not require this much bee power. The gardening beekeeper has two options: keep honey bees in traditional ways or keep bees in smaller, more "user-friendly" hives, non-traditionally.

Gardeners Keeping Honey Bees Traditionally. This technique is well established and all aspects of this text should be considered. Gardeners should know that beekeeping is not difficult, but does require an educational phase before becoming competent.

Gardeners Keeping Honey Bees Non-Traditionally. To date there is no standard honey bee garden hive design. The best application for a gardener is to employ a style of hive referred to as a nucleus hive within beekeeping. Such a hive is approximately 1/4 the size of a mature hive, is

easy to manage, and does not provide large populations of bees. Beekeepers commonly use this type hive to raise queen bees and to make colony splits. Both phases are considered temporary until the hive can reach full size. In the gardener's case, the colony remains within this domicile year-round.

1. **Advantages.** The hive remains small, by traditional beekeeping measures, and manageable. The hive does not require frequent management procedures and blends in the garden environment nicely. The potential for stings is greatly reduced.

Figure 54. A prototype garden hive with a side viewing door.

2. **Disadvantages:** Genetically, the colony is programmed to outgrow the nucleus hive. Probably one or two swarms per summer will depart from such small colonies. Swarming is a perfectly natural reproductive procedure that all healthy hives undergo. On average in the United States, a large colony will swarm once every other year. To a traditional beekeeper, a swarm represents a partial honey crop loss for that year. However, gardeners not having the same penchant for honey production, usually see an escaped swarm as a contribution to the wild honey bee population.

As the population grows, on warm days bees will hang on the front of the colony in a thick mat. Such bees are no more defensive than bees inside the hive, but the sight of so many bees hanging on the hive front can be disconcerting to the novice beekeeper. If crowded or on a hot day, bees will readily hang from the front of a full-sized colony.

Naturally, any hope of a significant honey crop can be forgotten when using a small hive. The bees literally have no space to store surplus honey. The nucleus hive does have the potential of having an extra box added during the production season in which surplus honey could be stored.

The Bee Skep. The bee skep is a bell-shaped woven basket that was used to house bees during the past century and is a decorative feature in many gardens. Though presently a common sight at craft shops, skeps were never widely used in the USA. Skeps are European in design and use. Though they might be quaint when stocked with bees in the garden setting, they violate common state beekeeping regulations in that they cannot be inspected for diseases and pests without destroying comb. Traditional beekeeping equipment has removable combs. Additionally, after a season or two of outdoor exposure, the skep takes on a weathered, unkempt look.

Figure 55. A woven skep. Sizes and shapes vary.

Status of Garden Hive Design. In all honesty, the international bee-keeping industry has never selected bees for anything but maximum honey production and population size. It would be possible to select for strains that do not reach large populations. Hive designs historically went through many years of evolution before arriving at its current position of imperfect perfection. Beehives tend to be plain and boxy, having nearly no style nor design left. From conversations with gardeners, the prototypic garden hive should have specific characteristics not commonly found in standard hives.

Characteristics of a Garden Hive:

1. Small when compared to traditional hives
2. Somewhat stylish and tastefully colored
3. Manageable from the outside of the hive (e.g. mite control regimes and occasional sugar feeding)
4. Stocked with gentle, low-swarming bees
5. Somewhat viewable (e.g. observational windows or viewing ports).

Although prototype hives with many of these features have been built, the perfect garden hive does not exist. The traditional nucleus hive, stocked with gentle bees, is the best alternative for the gardener wishing to keep small hives of bees. Such small hives will invariably swarm every year.

Gardeners and Bee Stings. It is an irrefutable fact that, under some conditions, bees will sting. It is the colony's defense mechanism. In general, about 10% of the colony's population is inclined to sting hive intruders. When stung, local swelling and pain is not considered to be life threatening. Maintaining small hives reduces the statistical odds of being stung. Common sense dictates that protective beekeeping clothing should be worn. Importantly, the queen should be replaced annually in garden hives to assure gentleness. The queen is the genetic reservoir within the colony. For many years, bee breeders have selected strains of bees for gentleness. Queens with this demeanor are readily available. Queens allowed to mate freely will normally exhibit more defensive offspring that a young queen that was commercially produced. Wearing protective clothing when performing actual bee manipulations and maintaining gentle stock within the hive can make the small hive a friendly addition to the garden environment.

Suggestions. Gardeners should look at bees as another crop within the garden, rather than an aspect of animal husbandry. Individual gardeners should decide to what level they wish to aspire in their beekeeping effort and with what kind of bees. If honey bees are selected, what size population is desired? In either case, the hive initiation procedure is the same. Secondly, the gardening beekeeper should be prepared to manage the queen during the spring of each year. This is not a difficult process, but does require minimal training and preparation. Thirdly, the garden beekeeper will need to employ mite control procedures and register with the state department of agriculture. If no honey production is desired, the springtime tasks of queen management and mite control will be the only required jobs. As with any gardening effort, a bit of good luck would be helpful. For gardeners having a bee interest, the chapters on starting hives, manipulating queen honey bees, and controlling honey bee mites should be reviewed closely.

CHAPTER 14

Transferring a Bee Colony from a Building or a Tree

Colonies frequently take up residence in the walls of houses, utility poles, empty 55-gallon drums, and discarded dresser drawers, even under an abandoned car's hood. Natural nests can be in nearly any place that is dark, dry and protected. Beekeepers are often asked to remove such unwanted colonies.

Figure 56. A wild bee colony in the wall of a house.

The Phone Call. When a call for assistance comes, a determination must be made whether it is honey bees, wasps or hornets causing the problem. Few beekeepers are interested in collecting any bee other than honey bees. People will tell nearly anything to get the beekeeper to the site. Deadly allergies, pending prom parties, livestock, children at play, and house painters on the job are common reasons people give when asking for immediate assistance. Transferring bees from a dwelling is a project that all beekeepers should try one time. Whether or not it is tried again will depend on how well the first effort proceeded.

Transferring bees should not be undertaken until the beekeeper is comfortable with bee behavior and biology. Some locations are simple and quick to remove while others may require getting into house attics or crawl spaces under mobile homes. Additionally, structural damage may be required in order to get to the nest site. Most beekeepers stipulate that they are not responsible for repairing the damage required to get to the nest.

[83]

Common Reasons for Transferring Bees from a Natural Nest Site

1. The beekeeper wants to increase his or her colony numbers.
2. The beekeeper wants to befriend the troubled property owner.
3. The beekeeper wants to befriend the bees.
4. Some combination of 1–3.

Two Procedures for Removing Bees from Natural Nest Sites

If the intention is to remove the bees and convert them to a productive colony, it should not be undertaken anytime except in spring or early summer. The trauma experienced by the colony will be massive and will require several weeks recovery time. Late in the year would not give the colony enough time to recover before winter.

The Cone Trap. The simplest, but slowest procedure, is to improvise a cone made of aluminum window screening and have an opening at the tip of about one-half inch diameter. The base is also open. The diameter of the base of the cone can vary according to the nest opening in the house or tree, but is usually around three to four inches. The cone is normally about ten inches long. The cone is stapled over the nest entrance. Upon leaving their nest, bees will walk down the cone, find the tip opening and fly away. However, upon returning from their foraging flights, they will be unable to find the tip opening and will gather at the base of the cone. As close as possible to the base of the cone, improvise a platform

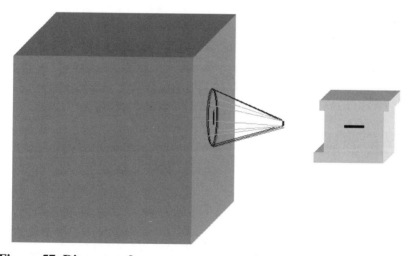

Figure 57. Diagram of a screen cone trapping bees out and directing them to a new hive.

and place a trap box having a couple of frames of comb containing a bit of honey and maybe a small amount of uncapped brood. Even better, would be to put a nucleus colony in the box headed by a queen. The bees, having been trapped outside, will quickly accept the nucleus hive, adopting it as their colony. The parent nest will continue to lose forager bees over several weeks time until it is too small to function. This process may take four–six weeks. After bees have stopped exiting the cone, the nucleus hive is removed for few days, as is the cone. Ideally, a small bee hive, either the same one or a different one, is placed back on the stand where its foragers will find the abandoned nest with its honey stores. They will rob it out and place the honey in the new hive.

However, the honey moving process from the old hive in the house to the newly relocated hive just outside the house only works if there is no nectar flow underway. If a natural nectar flow is ongoing, bees in the relocated hive will have little initiative to rob the old nest. Too much nectar is naturally available in the field. If this part of the process does not work and time is short, there is not much one can do except open the house up and remove honey and comb manually.

Figure 58. Beekeepers removing bees from the wall of a house.

Open the Nest Cavity. A more drastic procedure is, in fact, to open the nest cavity with whatever tools required. Generally, a saber saw or some other power saw is helpful. Secondly, a bee vacuum is used to pick up as many of the bees as possible (See Chapter 34, *Specialized Pieces of Beekeeping Equipment*). The bees will be flying all over, but they will quickly become demoralized and are not prone to sting. It is almost impossible to find the queen in this process. After as many bees as possible have been vacuumed, the next phase begins.

Once the nest is exposed, using a large knife, brood comb is cut away and is tied into empty brood frames. Simply wrapping the comb with cotton twine will hold the comb secure enough that the bees can glue it into place. Honeycomb is tossed into buckets and is moved from the area. Near the end of the task, bees are contained in the vacuum cage, honeycomb is in buckets, brood has been tied into frames, and remaining bees are flying all over. Fill the original nest cavity with insulation and board it back up. Improvise a platform next to the original entrance and dump the vacuumed bees onto the brood frames. This is a touchy moment. If bees settle down quickly and begin scenting, all is well. Lost forager bees will return to the site and accept the new colony. Have someone photograph this event for there is a good chance it will not be tried again.

Management of the Transferred Colony

After two or three days, during evening hours, move the transferred hive to its permanent site and look for signs of the queen (See Chapter 17, *The Honey Bee Egg*). The new colony will probably be weak. Feed the colony and treat for Varroa mites. After the colony has recovered from the move, put the brood combs that were taken from the original nest and position them towards the outside of the brood nest. As soon as they are empty, remove them and replace them with either comb or new frames.

CHAPTER 15

Record Keeping in the Apiary

Record keeping is not exciting and most beekeepers will not do it long term. However, for those who do manage to keep current, long-term records, the information generated becomes increasingly valuable and ultimately makes a better beekeeper. When do the first swarms arrive? When was the last swarm? When does the nectar flow begin and end in a given area. Whose equipment lasts longer? Where were the best queens purchased? Record keeping is not to be something done to the extreme, but keeping a written account of the bee operation is a tremendous improvement over what is normally used—a mental record.

In The Yard. Though many commercial beekeepers think of the individual yard as the single individual, hobby beekeepers should assign a number to individual colonies and maintain a profile of the characteristics and habits of particular colonies. Keep in mind that stinging bees and sticky honey may disrupt record keeping in the field. Therefore, any computerization of hive records will probably be done away from the hives.

Figure 59. The brick's position reminds the beekeeper of some hive need. In this case, the queen is not released.

There is no standard system of bee yard record keeping. Each beekeeper must employ a procedure that works for him or her. Records can be extensive or minimal. For many years, bee researchers at The Ohio State University used a large index card that had extensive categories for describing the activities of the queen and her brood, but little attention was given to honey production and swarming. The card was kept on the inner cover which had its center hole closed off. This was a convenient place for the card, but required permanently modifying the inner cover. Additionally the card could have been lost on windy or rainy days. Keeping the records in a simple box or notebook to be taken to the yard when needed would be safer. Various computer programs certainly have potential, however, most record keeping within the yard is recorded on note cards and notebooks.

A minimal record keeping system would include generalized comments on all aspects of the colony.

Suggested Entries for an Individual Hive Record Keeping

1. The queen (age and abilities, presence of brood, seasonal patterns, characteristics of offspring)
2. Presence of disease and subsequent treatment regimes (Terramycin applications, Varroa control procedures)
3. Swarming tendencies (stage of swarm cells, date observed and actions taken)
4. Honey production (when supers are added and removed, how many)
5. Colony manipulation (brood chambers reversed, supplemental feeding, entrance reducers installed, condition of combs and frames)
6. Extraneous information (unique equipment on the colony such as slatted racks or internal feeders and procedures used for controlling animal pests such as skunks; condition of equipment and need for maintenance could be noted)
7. Various reminders (grass cutting, matches and smoker fuel, or supply needs such as Terramycin, Varroa strips or sugar)

Record Keeping for the Beekeeping Business. Managerial record keeping is considerably different from business record keeping. Depreciation and inventory tables need to be established. Assets should be listed along with the date acquired, expected useful life, whether it was new or used, depreciation methods, investment credits, costs basis and salvage value should be listed. Additionally, profit and loss statements, capital sales and purchases, cash summaries, and operating income and expenses charts should be maintained. This type of information is easily computerized resulting in a quick, accurate assessment of the beekeeping business.

CHAPTER 16

The Honey Bees' Nest

Most beekeepers have misconceptions about the bees' nest. Many believe the beehive is composed of wooden frames, wooden boxes, and possibly some plastic foundation. In reality, all of these characteristics are beekeeper-derived and are not part of the bees' natural way of life. Due to mite predation, it is difficult to find wild honey bee nests today, but when the opportunity arises, look at the similarities and differences between a wild nest and a beekeeper-constructed domicile.

Figure 60. A colony nesting in the open.

When searching for a home, bee scouts usually look for a surprisingly small cavity, maybe as small as one cubic foot. The future bee home should: (1) be dark inside, (2) have a defendable entrance, (3) be dry, and (4) not have anything else living there such as birds, squirrels or ants. Ideally, it should not be on or in the ground. When tearing into trees, early beekeepers were confronted with a morass of bees, comb, brood, and dripping honey. How could any structure be found in something so chaotic? As known, the bee nest is a highly structured living environment. Understanding that structure can make one a better beekeeper.

The Population of the Nest. Wild nest populations and sizes vary significantly. The length of time it takes for a colony to fill a cavity varies greatly. Therefore, some nests are large, while others stay relatively small. Size variations could be due to: (1) genetics, (2) presence of diseases and pests, (3) the availability of nectar and pollen resources, (4) water resources, or (5) simple bad luck (tornadoes, lumberjacks, or the natural death of the host tree). In fact, as humans have altered the world's environment, suitable nesting sites are in short supply, thereby forcing bees to accept imperfect sites. A swarm is sometimes forced to build in the open, a fatal decision for most nests within the temperate parts of the USA.

The Nest Fixtures

The natural bee nest is furnished with wax combs only. Bees can modify the nest cavity to a degree, but they must accept the space as it is with little modification. Along the top and sides of the nest, surveyor bees will lay out the beginning midrib of combs, and other bees will begin to construct combs along those lines. While it is not understood how these surveyor bees measure out the spacing needed when laying out the dimensions for future combs, it was long ago discovered that bees require living and working space. The bee space concept allowed the subsequent development of artificial domiciles (See Chapter 2, *The Beekeeper's Equipment* for specifics on bee space measurements).

When bees first occupy a new nest cavity, the first matter of business is to construct worker combs and to set up housekeeping by getting a brood nest started. Besides being an area to nurse developing worker bees, worker-sized combs can also be used to store nectar, pollen, and occasionally water.

Combs seem to be produced almost mystically. The bees will mass together into a cluster. The cluster is fragile and temporary. As bees hang in a cluster, gravitational force causes it to hang perpendicular with gravity. In essence, combs are built in line with gravitational pull. Later, within the dark hive, this orientation with gravity becomes important in orienting the dance language communication procedure. Four pairs of wax glands on the ventral surface of the bee's abdomen produce virgin wax. Comb constructing bees pass a newly produced wax flake forward to their mouths where the wax is chewed and pulverized. After a short time, the wax particle is molded, using the bees' trowel-shaped mandibles, into part of a developing cell. It is a communal effort. Other bees may reshape previous efforts before adding their own contribution of wax to the new cell, but finally a new cell is produced. No single bee actually constructs a single cell. Experienced beekeepers have seen the completed cells in use near the top of a new frame while lower on the comb new cells will still be under construction. Bees build comb as needed. New wax is nearly snow white and is valuable for candles and other wax-produced products.

Cell Shapes. Individual cells are classic hexagons. Mathematically, this configuration provides the most strength and space efficiency of all common geometric configurations. The cell base is important in that it is not simply a flat plane, but is pointed so that each hexagonal cell base provides one-third of three cells on the opposite side of the comb.

Figure 61. View of a cell base showing thirds of three cell bases on the opposite side of the comb.

Figure 62. A comparison of honey bee cells with other common shapes. Hexagonal shapes are efficient in both space and building materials.

The Importance of a Nectar Flow. Inexperienced beekeepers are frequently disappointed that the bees do not use all brood chamber space and super space during a particular season. Indeed, beekeeper-supplied foundation may even be chewed and mangled by bees not building comb on it (though such damaged foundation will probably be successfully used during subsequent seasons). Bees will only construct comb on the impetus of a nectar flow and a space shortage. Simply stated, bees must have build-

Figure 63. A bee foraging for clover nectar.

ing material before they can build. Nectar provides that building material. It is an unusual building material since it is also stored as honey, rather than restructured into wax. Bees will not use stored honey to construct significant amounts of new comb. Again, the experienced beekeeper will provide drawn comb for the bees to store the crop rather than requiring bees to rebuild comb each year.

Comb is costly for the bees to build. It has been shown that bees must metabolize about 7–8 pounds of honey to produce one pound of wax. But with that one pound of building material, bees can build 35,000 cells in which they store 22 pounds of honey. Consequently, their approximate net gain after consuming 8 pounds of honey is 14 pounds of stored honey plus reusable comb. It takes about 10,000 bees over a three-day period to produce one pound of wax. That one pound will be made up of about 500,000 scales.[4]

Comb construction for the beehive is clearly an investment. Inexplicably, cappings and other wax particles are not reused to any

---

[4]Brown, Ron. 1981.

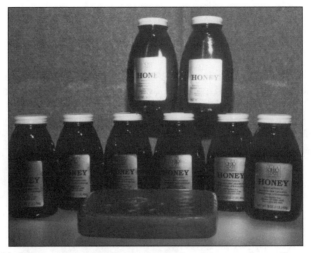

Figure 64. The amount of honey required to produce the wax cake.

degree, but are allowed to drop to the bottom board where they either accumulate or are discarded in front of the colony. New wax is soft and pliable and will break easily, but as the comb ages it becomes reinforced with old cocoons and propolis. New comb is snow white, whereas old comb is nearly jet black.

Types of Comb Cells within the Bee Hive. Worker comb is, by far, the most abundant comb size within the colony. Worker-sized comb (about 5 cells per inch) can be used by bees to house developing worker bees or to store honey and pollen. Larger cells, about four per inch, are used to produce drone larvae or to store honey and pollen. Distorted cells or cells of intermediate size can occur that are used by bees to splice worker combs together. In other words, worker comb will be filled with patches of drone comb with small amounts of transitional comb wherever needed. This is in order to make a piece of solid comb. Some cells may either be drastically modified or built purposefully for raising queens. As can be expected, this type of comb cell, though distinctive, is not particularly common within the combs. A modification of queen cells are queen cups that are simply queen cells that are not in use. Worker cells, drone cells, queen cells and transitional cells make up the types of comb within the colony.

Brace Comb, Burr Comb, or Ladder Comb. Bees will frequently build brace comb between frames, above or below frames, or on the bottom board, especially after a colony has been recently moved. Anywhere bee space is violated, additional distorted comb may be built, which is a nuisance to beekeepers in commercially manufactured hives. Normally, in managed hives, it is scraped off and melted as high quality wax. Within wild nests, it remains in place and helps give rigidity to the overall nest.

Figure 65. Large pieces of burr comb.

Inside the Warm, Dark Nest

Inside this dark maze of twisted, bee-spaced combs, the bees live in hot, humid darkness. Through the beekeeping years, innovative beekeepers have learned how to take the bees' penchant for building natural comb and have enticed them to build comb within wooden frames, mainly for human convenience. It is too difficult to remove cross-combed frames for honey removal, disease inspection, or colony manipulations.

Communication inside the Nest. Inside the warm, dark nest, bees probably communicate by smell (pheromone perception), touch, and other sensory perceptions such as gravitational sensitivity, and electromagnetism. It is also incredibly crowded. Bees are literally shoulder-to-shoulder. Yet, all these characteristics vanish when the beekeeper removes the top from the hive. The inside of the hive is visible. The normal behavior of the colony is disrupted by light and the application of the beekeeper's smoke. The visible hive is not the natural hive.

Chemical Communication. Within the undisturbed dark hive, everything has a unique odor. Workers, queen, drones, nectar, wax moths, brood, pollen, larvae's hunger, hive intruders, whether or not larvae are in the correct cell, everything seems to have an odor cue within the dark hive. Beekeepers use smoke to mask this elegant chemical communication. Temperature must be regulated to about 95°F in the brood nest. Nectar must be enzymatically reduced and excess water removed to form honey. The brood must be fed freshly collected pollen and honey. Hive-city must be defended from intruders and pests.

Figure 66. Orienting bees fanning air over their Nasonov glands.

Behavioral Communication. The best-known behavioral communication procedure is the bees' famous dance language. In fact, there are many types of dances that bees perform. The ones most interesting to beekeepers are the dances that bees use to find potential food, water, and home sites. The two most important dances are the wagtail dance and the round dance. Some of the information conveyed during a dance session is the odor of the source, direction to the source, distance to the source, taste, and an estimation of the richness of the source. Future research may show the presence of other unfamiliar factors such as magnetic or energy fields.

The Round Dance. If the food source is within eleven yards from the hive, the successful forager performs a "round dance." Essentially, the forager is saying that the food is near the hive and after giving the taste and smell of the source, the recruits take off searching in the vicinity of the colony. When a feeder is installed on the colony, confusion is caused by round-dancing bees sending recruits from the hive to find the source, while it is actually within the colony all the while.

The Wagtail Dance (The Waggle Dance). The wagtail dance is much more complicated, in that direction and distance are given during the dance process. The wagtail dance is in the shape of a compressed figure-8.

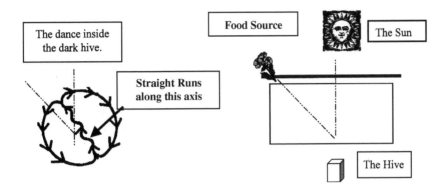

Figures 67 and 68. Dotted lines showing the dance angle (Left). The same dance angle on the comb (Right)

Obviously, bees cannot detect visible light within the dark hive. The upward direction is taken as being in the direction of the sun. Gravity's force is used to determine the upward direction. In the two diagrams above, take the angle of the straight run segment in the first as shown by the dotted line, and transpose the angle over the comb in the second figure. The diagram is showing that the food source is approximately 45° to the left of the sun. A recruited bee goes to the front of the hive, finds the sun and flies on a line that is 45° to the left of the sun for a distance given in the dance information. That distance is given in the dance by the number of straight runs given by the dancing bee in approximately fifteen-second intervals. About nine runs in the fifteen second period indicates a food source that is about 100 yards from the hive while only two straight runs in the a fifteen second interval would indicate a distance more like 1000 yards to the food source. A long interval between straight segment runs means a long distance to the food source.

The challenge to understanding this concept is that it is presented in writing in a 2-dimensional concept while it is actually a 3-dimensional event in the real world. In the examples presented above, to convert the angle in a different way, stand in front of the hive and face the sun. Point with the left hand at a 45° angle. The left hand will be pointing in the direction of the food source. The sun is the visual reference to the food source outside the hive. Inside the hive, the upward direction is used as a visual sun substitute in the dance behavior.

Deciphering this behavior resulted in the Nobel Prize being awarded to Karl von Frisch. It is a unique and complicated behavior. It makes bees highly efficient foragers. No other bee has such a system for efficiently sending recruits to profitable food sources.

The Bee Hive Society—The Caste System

This congested society must be kept in balance. In a full-strength colony, about 60,000 sterile workers and one fertile queen (the femaile caste system) and about 400–600 drones make up the population of a strong hive. Developing brood must be produced in anticipation of upcoming nectar flows or winter seasons. All these individuals come together to form the bee nest. Individual bees are incapable of supporting themselves for more than a few weeks under ideal conditions. The total bee nest is the animal—not the individual bee. Such is a day in the life of a bee in the nest.

Members of the Hive[5]

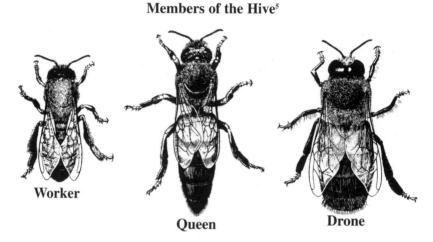

Worker

Queen   Drone

Figure 69. The three kinds of bees in the hive.

The Queen. The biology and behavior of the queen will be discussed in depth in Chapter 21. It is enough to say here that she is a unique bee within the hive. Even so, she would be nothing without the other two members of the honey bee system, workers and drones.

The Workers. Honey bee workers are sterile females, except for the secretion of specific pheromones and producing fertile eggs. These female workers do everything else within the hive. While honey bee queens may live for several years, honey bee workers only live for about 3–5 weeks in the summer and about twice that long during winter months. Queens and workers are diploid having 32 chromosomes.

---

[5]A USDA-produced diagram

Figure 70. Queen being cared for by workers.

Figure 71. Worker honey bees.

Worker Responsibilities.

After chewing her way out of her cell, she spends a few hours searching for food. She grooms herself and enjoys a brief period as a young bee. She may clean some cells, but essentially, she just sits quietly. This goes on for about four days, depending on the individual bee. She will feed brood until she is about ten days old after which time her brood food glands begin to shrink. From about twelve to eighteen days of age, her wax glands will be at full peak and she will be a comb builder. During this time, she will take play flights to learn how to orient and to learn the location of the hive. A need to defecate may be an underlying reason for taking the first flights. From about twelve–fifteen days of age, she serves as a house bee and receives nectar, pollen and water from returning foragers. She also processes nectar into honey and compacts pollen into cells. At about twenty-one days of age, when her venom sac is filled, she will serve either as a guard bee or as a forager. Some bees will guard for a bit and later take a foraging flight. Even so, the foraging stage is the last stage of life for the worker bee. There are no retirement programs.

Figure 72. Food sharing between two worker bees. This behavior distributes pheromones evenly throughout the colony.

The Drones

Somewhat like the queen, drones are specialized. The only real function they serve is to mate with unmated queens. (See Chapter 21, *The Queen—Her Biology, Production & Management*). The mating process kills the drones, but since large numbers of drones exist only to provide genetic variation, only a few are ever successful at finding and mating with a queen. Otherwise, drones sit in groups on the edges of frames and appear quiescent. They begin to take exploratory flights during mid-morning and

will retire for the day in the late afternoon. Drones are haploid (16 chromosomes) and are little more than flying gametes or flying sperm. Drones appear to live the perfect life within the colony, but they are the first to be eliminated during times of colony stress. Drone brood are commonly located near the edges of the comb where they are exposed to temperature extremes. During late autumn, drones are forced from the colony where they can be seen huddled

Figure 73. A drone honey bee beside a worker.

near the hive entrance. They soon die from exposure and starvation. During the late weeks of the following winter, strong colonies will once again begin to produce drones for the season. Weak colonies rarely produce drones unless they have a failing queen or laying workers (See Chapter 22, *Laying Workers and False Queens*)

Life History of Honey Bees

All members of the honey bee undergo complete metamorphosis. Queens, drones, and workers all spend part of their lives as eggs, larvae pupae and finally, adults. Due to the importance of eggs within the colony, a chapter has been allocated to this topic. All stages spend three days as eggs. Workers and queens spend about six days as larva while drones spend about seven days. Workers spend twelve days in the pupal stage. Queens spend seven days in the pupal stage, while drones spend about fourteen days in the pupal stage. Totaled, it requires twenty-one days for workers to develop, sixteen days for queens to develop and twenty-four days for drones to develop.

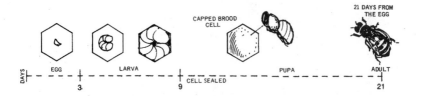

Figure 74. Development times for individual stages of the worker[6].

---

[6]Graphic from *4-H Basic Beekeeping Manual*, Ohio State University Extension (In press).

CHAPTER 17

The Honey Bee Egg

The eggs of the honey bee queen are useful management and decision making tools for the beekeeper. Their presence or absence can give the beekeeper much information about current conditions within the colony.

The Beginning. The beginning stage of a honey bee's life is the smallest and quietest of any of the four developmental stages being egg, larva, pupa, and adult. In fact, many beekeepers have problems even seeing eggs at all. Even the best of eyes can have problems seeing a tiny white egg (looking like a miniature grain of rice) standing on end in a cell of snow-white comb. An egg is not much longer than a typewritten dash ("-") (1/16") and is lightweight (0.12–0.22mg), which means an egg does not weigh much more than a typewritten dash either. Yet the presence or absence of eggs and their quantity, are good measurements of activities going on in the hive.

Figure 75. The honey bee egg.

Looking for Eggs under Field Conditions. First, one needs to get his or her mind attuned and eyeglasses adjusted to think small. With either dark or light comb, hold the comb at a 30-40 degree angle. Have the sunlight coming over one shoulder. Using the top bar as a pivot line, raise and lower the bottom bar about 3–5" randomly scrutinizing selected cell bottoms. Scan the comb bottoms. Eggs tend to be laid in patches of cells. When one egg is found, others can probably be seen in surrounding cells. Eggs are equally difficult to see in either color cell (light or dark). In dark cells, the polished cell bottom can glisten and look much like an egg. Alternatively, the while cell bottoms of new comb cells can

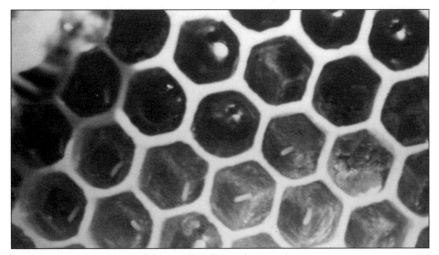

Figure 76. Eggs in comb.

camouflage the small white egg. Take heart, what seems impossible at first, does get much easier as the eye is trained.

Naturally, look for eggs in logical places within the brood nest. The center of the brood nest (normally the center of the hive) is the best place to look for eggs. However, suppose one is trying to decide how well a queen is performing or what kind of a future bee population the hive will have within the next few weeks. To determine that estimate, more than just seeing eggs in the center comb will be needed. Work from the center outwardly toward both sides of the colony. Be careful not to damage the queen. Under the crowded conditions of a late spring colony, there is a risk of rolling the queen off the comb if the center comb is removed first. How far out on either side were eggs or brood seen? If it is early spring and if capped brood and eggs on the center three frames are being found, then eggs on the next two frames (3–6 frames of brood), the beekeeper should have a colony that will build up on a normal build-up schedule. Anything more, and a boomer colony is probably going to develop while anything less may indicate a failing queen, bad weather, or low honey and pollen stores.

Most beekeepers will accept seeing eggs as a substitute for seeing the queen during a quick inspection. Since the egg stage lasts for three days, seeing eggs means that the colony had a queen in that colony at least three days ago. It is not a conclusive analysis, but it is quick and will satisfy most inspection needs.

No Eggs are Present. If no eggs are seen, under some conditions panic is in order. While in other situations, seeing no eggs at all is normal.

In climates having a cold winter, egg/brood production will completely stop during the coldest part of the season. If a colony is inspected during a warm day in that period, expect no eggs, ergo no brood. Nevertheless, one can assume there is a queen in place in the colony. Unless the queen is seen, there is no choice but to assume she is there. However, if winter is waning, eggs and older stages of brood are not being found, a failing queen should be suspected. Anytime after mid-winter, a colony should have varying amounts of brood in all stages.

Larva and Capped Brood are Present but No Eggs. The larval stage lasts about 5.5 days. Since larvae are present, the colony had a queen about 5–6 days ago. Was the beekeeper in the colony during those days? If the time of the year is right (anything warm), consider either swarming or supersedure as the reason. If all stages are present except eggs and the beekeeper's actions have been ruled out, the colony could have swarmed or could be replacing its queen. Swarm cells are generally on the bottom edges of the frame, while supersedure cells are on the "face" of a brood frame.

Time spent waiting for the new queen to show herself is a difficult period for many beekeepers. It is much like a surgeon saying, "We will not know how well the surgery went until the patients awakens." So how does one tell if the queen has shown herself? Look for eggs as described above. Once they are seen, get out of the colony. The queen is not in conclusive control of the colony until she has her own open brood present.

Laying Workers. Laying workers are worker bees that have had some ovarian development occur due to the absence of the hormonal effects of a fertile queen. Worker bees cannot mate or store sperm. They are also missing genital structures. Their egg patterns are messy and show multiple eggs per cell. Refer to Chapter 22 on laying worker behavior. There are other times when a colony with a perfectly good queen can have multiple eggs within single cells. If, at any time, the beekeeper introduces a strong, productive queen into a small, but biologically balanced colony, the queen's egg output may exceed the smaller colony's ability to provide cellular space for all the eggs. In that case, it is common for a queen to place 2 to several eggs per cell. But, in this case, all eggs are fertile and the colony is in no danger of collapse

Extra eggs within single cells are probably eaten by nurse bees, though not immediately. It may take several hours even to a couple of days for nurse bees to remove either dead or misplaced eggs. A more complete discussion of laying workers is presented in Chapter 22.

Egg Biology and Behavior. The egg is a hardy developmental stage of the bee's growth. It is attached with a secreted glue-like substance

Figure 77. Laying worker eggs.

by its small end. It is iridescent white with a gentle bend. The egg is positioned with the head-end up. After about three days, the egg gradually leans over, until it lies on its side on the cell base. The egg's outer membranous covering (the chorion) slowly dissolves as the larva emerges. It is a slow, quiet process. Nurse bees soon begin to place hypopharyngeal gland secretions (brood food) around and under the larva that has a voracious appetite. Beekeepers frequently say that an egg hatches when referring to a larva emerging. As such, the bee egg does not actually hatch, like bird eggs, though the word transfers the concept. However, due to the exterior membrane dissolution, do not ever expect to see tiny bee-egg shells dropping from cells containing new larvae.

Though the egg normally develops within three days, it is reported development range is 2–6 days. Temperature appears to play a role in the duration of the egg's development. Eggs can commonly withstand room temperature for several hours without the ill effects shown by larvae and pupae held under the same conditions.

Haploid (Drone) Eggs Compared to Diploid (Female) Eggs.
The egg is filled with cytoplasm, a nucleus, and a yolk. The nucleus is near the big end of the egg and plays a major role in the development of a future bee. A newly-fertilized honey bee queen will have nearly seven million sperm stored in a special pouch, the spermatheca. Sperm can be stored there, apparently in suspended state, for several years. Adult female worker bees cannot do this, hence a major difference between the anatomy and physiology of workers and queens. The adult, fertile queen has a muscular valve and pump which are used to withdraw a small amount of sperm from the spermatheca, pump it down the duct to an opening in the vagina

where a vaginal valvefold forces the egg's micropyle (an opening in the larger end of the egg) against the opening of the vaginal sperm duct. Once the connection is made, one or more sperm is passed into the egg. The newly-fertilized egg becomes diploid (a full chromosomal content) and develops into a female. Shut down the entire sperm-releasing mechanism and the egg remains sperm-free, resulting in a haploid egg (one-half of the chromosomal number). The unfertilized egg becomes a drone. A queen can seemingly tell a worker cell from a drone cell by measuring the cell diameter with her front legs and will deposit the appropriate egg. However, mistakes are occasionally made. Nurse bees, ever alert to errors, clean up the mistake by eating the errant egg.

The Egg Output of a Good Queen. How many eggs a good queen should produce is still inconclusive, though many estimates have been made. The most accepted estimate is 3000 eggs per day during the height of the egg-producing season. This is about twice the weight of the queen and is about 1,500,000 eggs for her entire career (a little less than three years). This estimate is dependent on many factors such as temperature, food availability (including pollen), and inherited characteristics.

Ironically, the view of the queen as a regal monarch is not a good one. The queen literally has food stuffed in one end while eggs are pushed from her other end. Probably about one egg per minute. Nurse bees can control the egg flow by controlling the queen's food input. Slow the food input and the egg rate drops. Other house bees are responsible for preparing cells for receiving eggs. Incoming nectar and pollen may also affect the egg flow by directly affecting the nurse bees that care for the developing brood. The queen systematically (if she is a good one by beekeeper standards) searches for prepared cells. Upon finding one, she puts the appropriate egg (drone or female) in the appropriate-sized cell. If she is not fed well or if clean and polished cells are not ready, she decreases egg laying proportionally, but it was not her decision to do so. If the queen cannot produce enough eggs when required, the same nurse bees will begin the supersedure process that will replace her.

CHAPTER 18

Honey Bee Stinging Behavior

The Sting

The honey bee sting is a modification of the female ovipositor, which is a structure used by some female insects to deposit eggs. Only females sting and that goes for all other bees and wasps as well. Isopentyl acetate, a chemical that smells like bananas, is released during the stinging process which sends an alert to other bees. Depending on the disruption and on the colony's temperament, these back-up bees may decide to sting also. The honey bees' defensive stinging system works well. People who do not keep bees logically think that beekeepers have some system, some bee magic, some procedure, and even some kind of tolerance for the occasional sting. Sorry, but this is not correct. Stings always hurt.

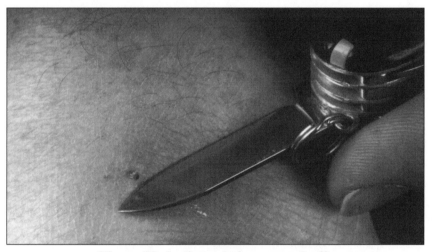

Figure 78. A stinger being scraped off.

Wearing all the protective clothing available to beekeepers will greatly reduce the chances of being stung; however, it is troublesome to put on all the required hot, protective equipment. At some point, the risk of a sting or two becomes less of a concern than the hot suit. Nearly all new beekeepers will begin to develop a tolerance to bee stings after receiving a few. Finally, the bee sting becomes nothing more than a short painful admonishment. Importantly, not all stings are the same. The age of the bee, the temperature of the day and the beekeeper's body temperature (stings hurt less during cold weather) all affect how the sting feels.

Swelling at the sting site is common and is not usually serious. Many people mistake this local swelling as a serious sting reaction and consider this a justification of why they will never be a beekeeper. A serious sting reaction is unmistakable. Difficulty in breathing, hives, swelling away from the sting site, fainting, and worse are all symptoms of a serious sting reaction. Thankfully, a reaction that only few people ever experience. The stinger tears out because the stinging bee is going to be quickly killed by the beekeeper and short-circuit the defensive sting effort. The bee sting system is ingenious in that the barbed stinger and venom sac tear away and will continue to inject venom in the victim. The barbed venom sac should be scraped out. It is frequently reported in the beekeeping litera-ture that grasping the stinger with the fore finger and thumb will only squeeze the venom in more quickly; however, this may not be true. Regardless, removing the stinger as quickly as possible is a common sense procedure that should be taken. A worker bee will die within a few hours of having her stinger torn out.

Bees can perceive movement quite well. An individual being attacked by a bee only gives the bee a better target if he begins to swat and flail around. All animals have an odor that bees can perceive. Angered bees will preferentially sting targets having two spots resem-bling eyes in deference to one spot or three spots. Bees can also perceive exhaled breath.

Suggestions for Avoiding a Bee Sting

1. In general, do not swat the bee.
2. If eyeglasses are worn, push them against the face with a finger, which will help them protect the eyes. Keep the head down.
3. With the remainder of the hand, cover the mouth and do not shout. This will offer some protection for the nose and mouth.
4. With the other hand, crush irate bees. Smash attacking bees, do not slap them.
5. All the while, keep moving away from the area—gracefully. Do not clumsily barrel along. Depart the area under control.
6. Be mentally prepared to be stung somewhere, but at least all the sensitive spots, which could be embarrassingly swollen the next day, have been protected.

Bee Venom. Bee venom is actually a potent chemical mix. It has enzymes like hyaluronidase and peptides like melittin. As a beekeeper progresses, he or she begins to lose the fear of stings, but never takes them whimsically. Moreover, be gentle with the people who do not keep bees. As a beekeeper, do not reassure the public with pretentious claims as to the number of stings that can be taken. On occasion, beekeepers have publicly proclaimed, *"I can take 400 stings! That'd kill an average man!"* Such comments do not reassure non-beekeepers and are not bene-ficial to beekeeping in general.

Serious Reactions to Insect Stings. While most people can withstand stings with only local swelling and pain, there are a small number of people who have violent reactions to even one bee sting. Experienced beekeepers should always watch themselves and others for symptoms of harmful sting reactions, such as difficulty in breathing or fainting. Another common symptom is itching away from the sting site. Remember that stings are intended to be painful, but even so, watch for reactions that appear to be more than local pain and local swelling.

Open Hive Demonstrations. When a beekeeper presents an open-hive demonstration, the public is comfortable so long as the beekeeper is comfortable. The ability to withstand a public sting with impunity is an invaluable asset for the public-minded beekeeper. If a beekeeper does not feel comfortable taking a sting or two, he or she should try not getting into a position where an inadvertent public sting causes an embarrassing episode, especially if the media is present.

CHAPTER 19

Honey Bee Anatomy

The Adult Bee

The bee, in all stages, is a physiological marvel, but then again so are all other insects. Whereas a worker bee only lives to be about three to five weeks, an amazing amount of physiological and mechanical processes are developed in the honey bee during that short time.

Three Body Segments

The honey bee, like all other insects, is made up of three body segments: the head, thorax, and abdomen. These features are not always evident in all insects, but they are always there. Each segment has specific assignments though there may be some overlap between systems such as the nervous system or the circulatory system. Body hair is one feature important to all segments. The bee is literally covered with hair. Bees' hair is branched (plumose), whereas human hair is straight-shafted. This hair covering is important in collecting pollen from flowers. Young bees are obviously hairy, while older bees may have a glossy black abdomen due to extensive hair loss.

General Honey Bee External Anatomy

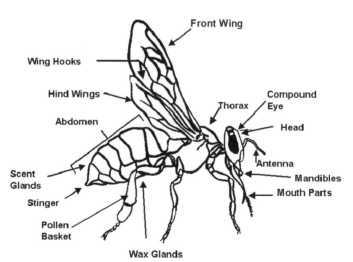

Figure 79. Major external parts of the honey bee.

The Head

Antennae. The triangular head is the frontmost part of the bee's body. On the head, two antennae are clearly visible and arise near the center of the bee's face. These appendages are freely moveable and serve as sensory organs. Bees use their antennae for functions such as wind speed determination, touch, and odor perception.

Eyes. The bee has two types of eyes, three simple eyes (ocelli) and two compound eyes. The function of the three simple eyes is still unclear, but they probably assist the bee in determining day length, thereby setting the bee's internal clock. They are located, in triangular fashion, on the top of the bee's head between the antennae. The two large compound eyes are positioned on either side of the bee's head and provide for general color vision. The compound eye is made up of about 3000 individual hexagonal-shaped facets. The bee's compound eye has a fixed focal length, i.e. the bee's eye cannot focus, as can human eyes. Bees can see the same colors as humans except for red; however, bees can see ultraviolet, which humans cannot.

Mouthparts. The mouthparts are made up of two mandibles (jaws) and a proboscis. The mandibles are used in several ways, primarily to mold and shape wax cells. The mandibles are also used for grasping anything needing to be carried or held. The proboscis is much like a common soda straw except it is not a permanent structure. Several individual structures are brought together by the bee to form a suction tube. When it is no longer needed, the individual structures are released and stored under the head between the mandibles. A muscular sucking pump lying in the head drives the proboscis. The proboscis is attached to the esophagus.

Glands. Several important glands are located in the head. The secretions of various glands, such as the salivary glands, hypopharyngeal glands, and mandibular glands, are important in brood feeding, queen feeding, and processing and ripening honey.

Thorax

The thorax is the bee's center of locomotion or the bee's engine room. All four wings and all six legs are attached to the thorax. The esophagus passes through the thorax, as do parts of the circulatory, respiratory, and nervous system. Unlike humans, bees do not have much of an internal skeletal system. The walls of the thorax serve as attachment points for muscles and other structures.

Legs. Honey bees have six jointed legs having the primary function of walking. Each set of legs has been assigned specific functions. However, all legs have the same kind of feet called tarsi. Primarily the bee's articulated foot is made up of two large claws with a spongy, sticky pad between them. When a bee walks on surfaces like plant or hive surfaces, she predominantly uses her claws for holding on to the rough surface.

However, when she walks on a smooth surface like glass, her claws push backward, allowing the sticky pad to cling to the smooth surface. Many insects have taste structures on their feet so they taste food as they walk on it.

Front Legs. Other than walking or grasping, the major feature of the front leg is the antenna cleaner. This structure is a deep semicircular notch on the inside middle portion on the leg and has a spine that can be closed over the notch. The notch is lined with short, stiff hairs. When cleaning antenna, the bee places the antenna in the notch, squeezes her front leg closed and pulls the antenna through the notch where the short hairs clean them. Since antennae are sensory structures, it is important to the bee that they stay clean and functional.

Middle Legs. The primary specialized structure on the middle leg is a stiff spine useful in transferring wax scales from the bottom surface of the bee's abdomen. Other than this responsibility, the middle leg performs only the standard functions.

Hind Legs. The hindmost leg is highly modified to serve as a pollen transporting structure. Essentially, the pollen foraging bee—covered in hair—combs pollen from her body using various hair-combs on all her other legs. She lightly moistens this pollen with nectar making it sticky with a tendency to clump. These small pollen clumps are passed to the rear legs where specialized rakes, again made of stiff hairs, are used to assemble them into a larger ball, which is packed onto the outer surface of the rear leg. The bee smooths and shapes the collection of clumps into a compacted ball of pollen called a pollen pellet. A single long, still spine serves to reinforce the pellet while it is being transported back to the hive where both pellets from each leg are unloaded into a cell where a house bee packs it into the back of the pollen cell.

Wings. Bees have four wings, two large front wings and two smaller back wings. Wings are thin membranous appendages containing no muscles. Veins that provide reinforcement support the thin wing structures. Before a bee can take flight, she must hook the back wings to the front wings using a small row of marginal wing hooks along the front margin of the back wings. In flight, a bee uses two large wings rather than four smaller wings. When at rest, the wings are unhooked and folded back over the thorax and abdomen.

Wings provide lift when powered by muscular vibrations of the thorax. Picture a child's seesaw but put the fulcrum off center. Now picture muscles being attached to the short end of the see saw and the long end being the wing. When the thorax contracts, flight muscles pull the wing up. When other longitudinal muscles contract, the wing is pulled down.

Obviously, this all happens rapidly. Flight is much more complicated than what has been discussed. Only lift has been described. Directional changes require different wing positions just as a helicopter requires some method of moving forward not just upward.

Diagrams of Bee's Attachment and Movement of Wing Muscles[7]

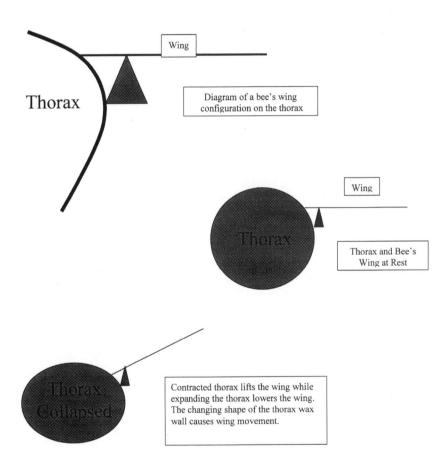

Figure 80. Diagram of bee wing movement.

---

[7]Diagrams are made as though one is looking at the bee from the front through a cross-section of the thorax. Only the left wing is shown in the diagram.

The Abdomen

Exterior. The abdomen is the bee's cargo bay. It contains the body organs and the honey sac. It is the rearmost segment of the bee and is comprised of hard interlocking plates much like armor. Except for external openings to the respiratory system, there are not many external features. While plumose hair is present, the abdomen of the bee is not as hairy as the head or thorax.

Interior. The abdomen contains the respiratory system, the circulatory system, the digestive system, the nervous system, and the reproductive system. Except for the reproductive system, some parts of each of these systems can be found in other segments, but the major parts are abdominal.

Glands and Organs. On the outer surface of the abdomen, eight wax glands (four pairs) are found on the bottom surface of the bee's abdomen. Naturally, these glands are important for comb production. The scent gland is located at back tip of the abdomen. This gland is useful to beekeepers in determining when bees have accepted a new hive or a new home site. The pheromone produced by the scent gland is important in telling other bees that a particular site or source has been discovered. When the scent gland is exposed, the bee puts the tip of her abdomen up and fans air across it attracting other bees. The sting apparatus is contained within the bee, but as beekeepers know, the sting lancets are pushed outward when the sting is required for defensive purposes (See Chapter 18, *Honey Bee Stinging Behavior*). The reproductive system of both drones and queen bees is contained at the back of the abdomen. In workers, the reproductive system is essentially non-functional, but is important in both drones and queens. The rectum lies along the upper side of the abdomen and is capable of expanding greatly during times when the bee cannot relieve herself. Rectal storage is important for wintering bees so they can go for several weeks without relieving themselves.

On the front end of the abdomen, the esophagus is modified to form the elastic honey sac. The sac (crop) has specialized valves on either end in order for the bee to restrict food movement into the digestive system and to assist with cleaning the nectar. The honey sac is used to transport nectar back to the hive for processing into honey.

Honey Bee Anatomy Overview

Although the internal and external structures of the honey bee are complex and specialized, beekeepers should realize that honey bees are no more complicated than many other species of insects. Since beekeepers specialize in honey bee biology and management, particular structures and features are important to understand. The information presented here is only intended to introduce the beekeeper to the marvels of honey bee anatomy. More advanced sources are available for the beekeeper needing additional information.

CHAPTER 20

Water Needs in the Hive

Bees foraging in the neighbor's pool and bird baths. "How do I keep my honey bees away from my neighbor's swimming pool?" is a commonly asked question. Until the arrival of Varroa and tracheal mites, beekeepers could say that they were not sure that the bees were from their hives. Nowadays, the chances are excellent that honey bees from managed hives are the ones seen around a neighbor's swimming pool. Water sources as large as a swimming pool: (1) have both an odor and taste, (2) are easily visible, (3) do not dry up, and (4) would be large enough to establish a "humidity field." When bees visit the neighbor's pool, they train themselves to specific watering sites at the pool that are frequently on or around the pool ladders. These make good places from which to stand while drinking. There is not much a beekeeper can do, except provide a dependable water source, provide it near the hive, and never, never let it dry up. If this fails, the colonies may have to be moved.

Figure 81. A forger collecting water from a flower pot drain hole.

Bees foraging for water at feedlots. Bees can frequently be seen foraging for water and minerals at unsavory locations such as feedlots. The fact is that bees do not always look for the cleanest sources of water. They will readily collect from manure pits, stagnant pools or other questionable water sources having nitrogenous byproducts or trace minerals that bees need. Obviously, the physical size of many undesirable water sources, combined with the smell and taste, would make such a site much easier for a water forager to find when compared to a drum or some other manageable container of clean water. Consequently, bees probably have more difficulty locating and collecting from a small, clean water supply. While they collect from a clean source, foraging bees will expose their Nasonov gland (the scent gland) in order to help other bees find the same source. Honey's redeeming feature is that it has a novel system for safeguarding against such nastiness—naturally occurring hydrogen peroxide within honey. In addition, honey has a low moisture content that will desiccate microscopic invaders. Consequently, honey is, by its nature, a clean product. Even so, consider moving colonies that are collecting from suspicious sources. However, one never really knows where all the other water-collecting sites are.

Why bees drink. Thirsty bees forage for water for many of the same reasons that people need water. They need water for themselves, for their developing young, and to cool the hive during hot weather. The hive reception procedure is interesting. Water foragers probably make the decision to collect water individually. Maybe an individual bee is hot and simply went out for a drink. Regardless, if house bees at the hive entrance eagerly meet water foragers and the water is quickly unloaded, water foragers are stimulated to make more water foraging trips. If such tanker bees are unloaded within 60 seconds, they take off on another flight for more water. Anything longer than 60 seconds discourages water collection and unloading times longer than 180 seconds will outright stop water collection. Controlling the internal hive temperature is critical for the colony's development of immature bees. In hot weather, bees collect water and put it in indentations in the burr comb along the top bars and within cells near brood. Bees, fanning their wings, evaporate the water thereby cooling and humidifying the hive. Bees given the task of holding water until needed have been dubbed reservoir bees. They stand quietly near the brood areas and dispense water as needed. They serve a particularly important function for providing water during hot nights when foraging is not possible. Hive nurseries are kept in the range of 94° –96°F. As temperatures increase to 96°F and above in the brood area, the demand for water increases. Initially, nurse bees deposit the contents of their crops in a thin film into or near brood cells. If these procedures still do not bring rising temperatures under control, nurse bees and house bees begin to eagerly search throughout the hive for bees having crop contents of dilute nectar or even better—plain water. That would leave foragers having good, sugar-laden nectar loads standing idle while bees with lesser sugar contents or ideally water are suddenly in demand. Communications within the hive swing toward using the foraging force to collect water. Finally, temperatures drop, and attention again shifts to either pollen or nectar collecting bees.

Frequently, during these periods, the majority of the adult bee population will completely move out of the hive, a sight frequently seen in parts of the southeastern and southwestern USA. During these times, bees will mass around the entrance of the hive giving the few remaining bees inside the colony more space to evaporate water and cool the bee nursery. Additionally, by removing so much body mass, internal hive temperatures will drop. For many parts of the USA, 96°F and higher is not an uncommon daily temperature. The need for water collection is daily or even hourly. Unemployed bees are nearly always hanging outside the hive. It is an excellent idea to provide bees water within the hive during such hot weather. Common Boardman feeders, pail feeders, division board feeders or even animal waterers such as those used to water chickens are excellent ways to get water to the bees. In hot climates, staggering supers in order to allow for upper level ventilation, will make evaporation more efficient and help in keeping the colony cooler. Beekeepers have occasionally pointed out that so many extra openings may incite robbing of weaker colonies. This is true, but weak colonies are at risk anyway. Hot bees are not friendly bees; they are defensive bees and would be on guard to prevent robbing.

It should also be known that bees are not always collecting water because the hive is hot. Bees commonly collect water because they need it to dilute honey in order to feed it to developing bees. Bees can also use metabolic water or water produced as a physiological byproduct. During cold months, water for brood can be obtained from either frost or ice within the colony.

Bees need abundant supplies of water all year and if not provided for them, they will find it elsewhere. Let a faucet drip, provide an internal water supply, keep a bird bath filled nearby, install a fish pond, or buy a plastic child's swimming pool, but by all means, keep the water sources wet. Once bees dry out, they will move to other sources.

Bee Hive Water Facts[8]

1. Time for a bee to load up—1 minute
2. Normal time for the water run—3 minutes or less (67%), 10 minutes or less (92%).
3. Rest period between trips—2–3 minutes
4. Water trips per day—50 (100 max)
5. Average water load—about a drop
6. One quart of water will take 800 bees working all day
7. Daily water use per colony—around 1/2 pint–2-1/2 pints

---

[8]Park, O.W. (1923). Behavior of water carriers. *American Bee Journal 63:553*

CHAPTER 21

The Queen—Her Biology,
Production & Management

Biology. The queen is often seen as the most important individual within the colony and indeed, as an individual, she probably is. The queen functions in two major ways within the colony. First, she is responsible for all brood production consequently directing the colony's genetic characteristics. Second, she is responsible for producing chemicals (pheromones) that stabilize the colony by making her presence known to all the other bees in the colony.

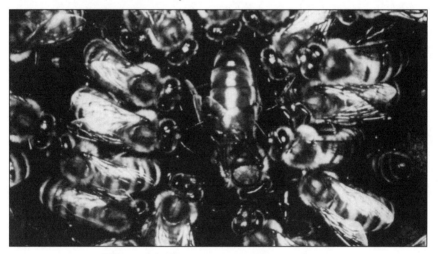

Figure 82. The queen and her retinue.

For the first three days of its larval life, any worker bee within the colony could become a queen bee if she is fed a different diet more nutritious than the regular worker bee developmental diet. By the fourth day, the larva will have been selected as either a worker or a queen bee.

Qualities of a Good Queen. The colony's queen is the genetic reservoir for the colony. Though beekeepers like a pretty queen (by human standards), physical appearance is not nearly as important as the characteristics she imparts to the workers and drones within the colony. Therefore, the attributes of the colony should be based on an overall evaluation of the colony—not just the queen's demeanor. A good queen will have a concise brood pattern located near the center of the colony. Except for occasional drone brood, brood will not be scattered about on various frames. Within the brood pattern, a queen with good cell-searching behavior will miss only the occasional cell. In the laying pattern of a good queen, there will actually be the perception of concentric circles of brood —indicating that the queen systematically worked the frames on multiple days.

Naturally, her offspring should be gentle, productive, and winter well. Beekeepers like bees to be quiet on the comb and not great propolis users. Good bees should show all these characteristics. Beekeepers also like bees to be pretty and robust-looking. Some beekeepers like dark bees while other beekeepers like bright orange bees.

Figure 83. A queen cell next to drone and worker cells.

Queen Cell Production and Development. A colony will follow three instincts that result in queen production: supersedure, emergency cell production, and swarming. In cases of swarming or supersedure, specific cells will be constructed that faintly resemble peanuts suspended from the face of the comb. Emergency queen cells are modified worker cells that will look similar to mature (ripe) swarm or supersedure cells. Unlike workers and drones that undergo larval development while lying horizontal in the cell, the queen develops hanging head-down. The queen is an egg for three days, a larva for six days, and a pupa for seven days taking a total of sixteen days for the queen to complete her development from egg to adult.

Mating Behavior. Upon emerging, a virgin queen will roam the colony searching for other virgin queens or for queens still encased within their cells. Occasionally, virgin queen will make a high-pitch pulsating sound that beekeepers call "piping." Other virgins may respond by piping. They will meet on the comb, and a battle to the death will follow. Queens still encased within their cells, but completely developed, will also make a muted version of the queen battle sound, called "quacking." Such queens are usually killed within their cells for giving away their location. Worker bees remove the bodies of dead queens and destroy the remnants of queen cells leaving the colony with one virgin queen.

After adult queens mature for five to six days, they take their nuptial flights. On warm days when the wind is still, queens will make orientation flights that will take from five to thirty minutes. When taking mating flights, queens fly to Drone Congregation Areas (DCAs), which are aggregations of drones from colonies within the area. Drone Congregation Areas limit inbreeding in the bee colony and may be made up of thousands of individual drones flying randomly within the area searching for the rare queen. Queens may take one or a series of flights in the process, mating with twelve to twenty drones. The selection of drones for successful mating appears to be random and occurs while the drone and queen are in flight. The process kills the drone and he drops to the ground leaving a "mating sign" attached to the queen. Each drone deposits about 6–10 million spermatozoa within the queen's oviducts. After returning from her mating flights, during the next forty hours, about 4–7 million of the sperm deposited by the drones will actively move to the queen's spermatheca where it will be stored for the next two to four years. Eggs that are fertilized (diploid) will produce either workers or queens, while eggs that are not fertilized (haploid) will produce drones. About three days after the mating process is over, the queen begins to produce viable eggs. Once at this stage, the queen will never again mate.

Figure 84. Instrumental insemination of a honey bee queen.

Instrumental Insemination of Honey Bee Queens. Honey bee queens can be microscopically fertilized using very specialized queen-holding equipment and a microscope. Sexually mature drones are sacrificed and semen is collected from them. This is a complex process requiring training and costly equipment, but this is the only way the parentage of a queen can be guaranteed. Honey bee geneticists and queen breeders will frequently use this procedure when developing special lines of bees for breeder queens.

Breeder queens are individual queens producing offspring that have desirable characteristics. Breeder queens can be either naturally mated or instrumentally inseminated. Breeder queens produce the young larvae that beekeepers use for grafting queens. The offspring produced by breeder queens, referred to as line queens, are the familiar queens mailed to beekeepers. (See The Breeder Colony later in this chapter.)

The Queen's Career. During her one- to two-year lifetime, a good queen can produce 1000 to 1500 eggs per day during the brood-rearing period and will lay about 200,000 eggs per year. Though queens can live for several years, they are at their best production capability during the first year and will frequently lead a swarm during the second year. Normally after the swarm has found a new hive and egg production begun, the old queen will be superseded. While a bit risky, annual requeening is a good idea if the output of the colony is to remain strong. Except for the rare swarm, after taking her mating flights, the queen will never again leave the colony.

Requeening a Colony. The principles of requeening a colony, for any reason, are similar in all cases. From human perspective, one would think that the colony would be grateful for the sudden appearance of a queen when the colony has lost all hope of producing one on its own. This is very wrong. Without a proper introduction process, bees within the hive will immediately kill a new queen. Reasons for this hostility to foreign queens are unclear. A colony can be requeened at any time during the year, but a hard winter would obviously be a difficult time for requeening in most climates in the United States. Most requeening occurs in the spring when populations are low and a nectar flow is underway.

The Requeening Process. An incredible number of procedures have been described for requeening a colony. Wetting the queen with water, shaking all the bees out front of the hive and dropping the new queen amongst the bees as they return to the colony, or putting ripe queen cells in supers are four diverse procedures that have been employed at one time or another to introduce foreign queens to a new colony.

The traditional procedure requires a small, screened cage having two openings—one that is plugged with a cork and the other plugged with sugar fondant and an external cork plug. Plastic plugs may replace the cork plugs on some cages. The queen is confined with about six attendant bees in the cage. In the colony, the old queen is found and removed. Though some beekeepers may say to wait a day or so before positioning the caged queen in the colony, most beekeepers put her in the hive immediately. Unless the queen is to be manually released later, the cork plug restricting the candy plug should be removed exposing the candy plug to worker bees. The cage is positioned between top bars with the screened side exposed to worker bees in the brood nest area. The candy plug is usually put toward the bottom of the hive. Approximately three to four days later, the cage should be gently removed using only a little smoke to quiet the bees. If the queen has not been released and the bees appear gentle, the queen should be physically removed from the cage. At this particular time, the queen can actually act silly by human standards. She may cower in the cage and refuse to leave the cage. Worse, she may immediately fly from the cage. Even though this does not happen often, it does happen. If this is experienced, leave the hive open and move away from it. Ideally, the lost queen will be attracted to the odors of the open colony. Once the queen has run down into the colony, quietly close the hive. Check the colony two to three days later to be sure she was accepted and that she is laying.

Sometimes things go wrong and the reasons may not be clear. Maybe the queen is defective in ways not seen. Unfortunately, the occasional queen may be unacceptable. At that point, decide if another queen can be ordered in time to save the colony or if the colony should just be combined with another. However, this risk of introduction failure should not prevent requeening when needed. While there is a risk of queen introduction failure, the greater risk of lost honey crops, swarming, or supersedure is more serious.

Figure 85. Caged queens with attendant bees.

Producing Honey Bee Queens. An in-depth discussion of queen production is beyond the scope of this book, but enough should have been said to help the beginner initiate a new phase of beekeeping—queen production. Of the three stimuli for raising queens (supersedure, swarming, and emergency), nearly all queen producers use the "emergency" stimulus to initiate queen cell production. The emergency is caused by abruptly removing the queen from the parent unit requiring the colony to produce a new queen as rapidly as possible. Depending on the procedure, anywhere from a few to several thousand queen cells can be produced by a strong queenless colony.

Of the myriad methods of queen production, the most commonly accepted is the Doolittle method of queen production or some variation of it. (See page 123, The Modified Doolittle System of Queen Production.) If used to maximum production, the Doolittle method requires four types of colonies: the breeder, the cell builder colony, the cell-finishing colony, and the mating nucleus. For the beekeeper who only wants to produce a few queens, the full production of this system would swamp the small operation. By modifying the procedure, a smaller number of queens can be produced with reduced equipment requirements. All colonies should be fed sugar syrup during the queen rearing process.

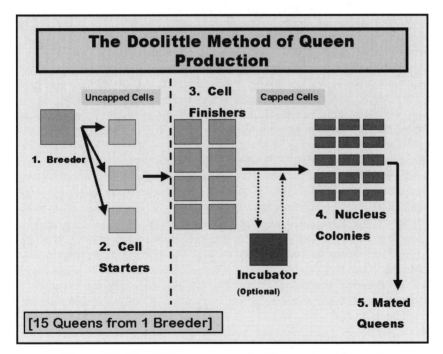

Figure 86. Doolittle queen production system[9] layout.

[9]Doolittle, G.M. (1915). *Scientific Queen Rearing*. American Bee Journal. Hamilton, IL 62341

The Breeder Colony. In large operations, the breeder colony is the genetic source of all the queens to be produced. In effect, the breeder queens produce perfect bees—ones that beekeepers wish all queens were like. However, on a smaller scale, the breeder colony can be a practical matter of which colony has larvae the right age for grafting or which colony produced the most honey the past year.

The Cell Builder. Normally housed in a single deep brood chamber, the cell builder is a queenless, populous colony having abundant food and capped brood but no eggs or uncapped brood. If this colony had access to eggs or uncapped brood, it would attempt to produce natural queen cells and ignore the grafted larvae. One-day old larvae are transferred (grafted) to wax or plastic cell cups and are placed in the Cell Builder. Grafting needles, tooth picks, brazing rods, and artist paint brushes have been used to pick up the tiny larvae for transferring. Make no mistake, this is a tedious process but one that can be learned quickly. About 10–35 larvae are grafted at once. For whatever reason, if grafting is out of the question, various devices such as the Jenter[10] Queen Rearing Device can be used to entice the queen to put eggs on plugs that can be moved to the cell-building colony without having to pick up the small larvae.

Twenty-four hours later, a quick review of grafted cells will tell which were accepted and which were neglected. Accepted cells will have fresh food surrounding the larva and construction will have begun on the cell. At this point, the cells can remain within the colony until they mature (about twelve days) or they can be transferred to Cell Finishing Colonies.

The Cell Finishing Colony. From a bee resource perspective, cell-building colonies are expensive to maintain. They must be kept strong and have a constant source of capped brood with accompanying nurse bees. This colony can not provide these resources for itself, so other colonies must be parasitized to get the needed bees, brood, and food. Cell Finishing Colonies are nothing more than strong queen-right colonies having the queen confined below an excluder. Above the excluder, young bees and frames of capped brood are positioned with frames of uncapped queen cells between them. These young nurse bees will finish maturing the cells. About 35 cells can be completed by a single finishing colony. The use of finishing colonies frees up the cell builder colony so it can be used repeatedly. Ten days after the cells were grafted, they must be taken from the finishing colony and put into their final site.

The Incubator. The incubator is not a component of the original Doolittle process and is not required. Many times, queen producers raising

---

[10]Jenter Queen Rearing Device available from Brushy Mountain Bee Supply, 610 Bethany Church Road, Moravian Falls, NC 28654

large numbers of queens will need to hold the mature cells for a day or so before being able to put them in queen mating nucs. Commercial incubators range from simple heated boxes to complicated thermostatically-controlled units.

The Mating Nucleus Hive. If mated queens are the goal, a mating nucleus is used to install the ripe queen cell, allow her to emerge, take nuptial flights and begin egg production in the nucleus hive. A nucleus hive can be small, having only a cup or so of bees (baby nucs), or as large as 5-frame nucleus hive. The larger the nucleus, the more bees required to stock it, but the larger the nucleus hive, the easier it is to maintain it as a small hive. Many times, ripe queen cells are used to requeen production colonies. The ultimate use and the type of mating unit are determined by the individual beekeeper.

Figure 87. Queen mating nuclei.

The Modified Doolittle System of Queen Production

If only a few ripe queen cells are required, the Cell Builder and Cell Finishing can be combined. Normally, ten to thirty-five grafted cells would be given to the queenless unit and ten days later, the ripe cells would be removed. The important point for producing queen cells is that a strong colony is made queenless and has neither eggs nor larvae for producing another. At that point, the beekeeper provides selected larvae to the queenless unit. Since virgin queens will kill each other, just before they emerge ten days later they are removed and used for multiple beekeeper reasons.

Queen Cell Producing Devices. Several special cages have been developed for beekeepers during recent years. Though each model is somewhat different, each device requires that the queen be confined to a plastic cage approximately four inches square. A hole large enough to contain the plastic cage is cut from a piece of drawn comb. The cage, having a grid covering, is placed in this hole. The grid allows worker bees to enter and exit but contains the queen within the cage. The queen is forced to lay in approximately one hundred specialized cells. These cells have a removable base. The cell base, holding the egg, can be detached and transferred to a companion plastic cell that mimics a queen cup. In essence, the queen is forced to put eggs in special cells that beekeepers can move to starter colonies without having to graft larvae so the grafting requirement is eliminated. All this sounds much more complicated than it is. Actually, these devices work well.

There are entire books written on queen production. Nearly everything in queen production can be modified or changed to meet individual beekeeper needs. The methods described here are only to introduce the beekeeper to the rewarding area of honey bee queen production.

CHAPTER 22

Laying Workers and False Queens

Laying Workers

Laying workers are surprisingly frequent in the beehive. There can be one or several. Worker bees cannot mate or store sperm so they cannot produce viable eggs. They are also missing genital structures and some behavior patterns of fertile queens. Since laying workers cannot fertilize eggs, any unfertilized eggs produced will become drones; therefore, it is impossible for an adult worker bee to become a true, fertile queen. Diploid or fertilized eggs (32 chromosomes) become either queens or workers, while haploid or unfertilized eggs (16 chromosomes) only become drones (males). Unfortunately, males do not contribute much more than reproductive activities to the colony. After a colony becomes hopelessly queenless, laying workers will generally develop within 23–30 days or so. A major indication of the presence of laying workers is multiple eggs within single cells—all of which will ultimately become small drones. Since the laying worker's abdomen is shorter than the queen's abdomen, she cannot reach the bottom of the cell, so she deposits her eggs along the sides of the cell—a classic symptom of laying workers. Laying workers will require up to 1 minute to deposit an egg whereas a true queen will perform the same task within seconds. Additionally, fertile queens can produce thousands of eggs per day while a laying worker can only produce a few hundred. Laying workers are able flyers and will even continue to take occasional forging trips as though they were normal foragers. These bees can easily find their way back to the original colony location.

By the time the colony has dealt, unsuccessfully, with its queenless situation (about 30 days), it will have become noisy (excessive orientation fanning when the colony is opened), nervous, and possibly a bit defensive. The colony will be weak and its hive members old. It is probably not worth saving, but it will have eggs all over the brood nest area. In this case, abundant eggs in cells are not an indication of a productive queen.

To some extent, laying workers are thought to be present nearly all the time within the productive hive, but the activities of a normal queen and the supporting activities of house bees keeps all the improper eggs removed. Therefore, the presence of laying workers goes unnoticed.

False Queens

An advanced condition can arise where an individual laying worker has become so well established that she carries herself as *false queen*. Her abdomen will be slightly enlarged and she will be calmer on the comb, but her progeny will still be runty drones.

Laying Worker Drones. Drones produced by laying workers are usually small and stunted. These drones are frequently undersized and may not be useful in mating natural queens or in any other managerial way providing normal drone functions for the colony. However, many drones produced by laying workers do produce viable semen.

Salvaging Laying Worker Colonies. Due to the declining strength of colonies having laying workers, such colonies are notoriously weak and rarely worth saving. Even so, beekeeping management justifications vary greatly and many beekeepers do attempt to save affected colonies. Forget common requeening procedures. As far as the afflicted colony is concerned, it has a queen; therefore, most of the time, newly introduced queens will not be accepted. By far, the most common recommendation is to simply combine the laying worker colony with another stronger colony. The laying workers will be amalgamated with normal worker bees in the new colony and will lose their physiological interest in being the colony's queen.

A technique that may occasionally be of value in attempting to requeen a laying worker colony is to shake all bees into a shipping cage containing a new caged fertile queen. Leave them confined with the new queen for two or three days while keeping them well-fed and calm. Then release the bees back into the hive equipment and install the queen in traditional ways. Though still not great, the chances are improved that the new queen will be accepted.

CHAPTER 23

Honey—Its Production, Processing and Packing

Though nearly everyone appreciates the services that pollinating honey bees provide, the delectable honey crop has always given honey bees their special place in the bee world. Honey is a high-carbohydrate food. It is heavy and sticky, but it is always in demand as a quality food.

In the United States, honey is produced primarily in the springtime with many areas also getting a fall nectar and pollen flow. Generally speaking, the spring honey crop is more palatable than the fall crop that may have a more pronounced flavor. In reality, there is rarely a pure honey crop of only one nectar source. Specific honey flavors like Alfalfa, Clover, or Basswood honey are promoted, but such crops are rarely pure monoculture nectar sources. This does not mean that honey producers are not being truthful, but rather that the advertised crop is predominately from a particular nectar source or sources. Light-colored honey crops are preferred over darker varieties of honey.

Figure 88. A full deep frame of honey.

Honey crops generally come from obvious nectar sources like clover, orange blossom, almond, or fireweed; however, there are thousands of minor nectar sources that contribute as nectar sources. Taken individually, minor nectar sources rarely result in a honey crop, but combined minor nectar sources can be a major nectar source for bees.

The Composition and Characteristics of Honey

Ninety-five percent of the solids in honey are carbohydrates in the form of simple sugars or monosaccharides. Two of the major sugars in honey are glucose and fructose. Complex sugars such as sucrose, lactose, and maltose, are also found in honey. Listing these few sugars may leave the false impression that honey is just a simple mixture of common sugars, but in fact, honey is a highly complex sugar mixture.

In addition to sugars, honey is acidic having an average pH of 3.9. This acidity can cause the human honey consumer a slight burning sensation in the back of the throat. Minerals are also present in honey in small amounts, about 0.17% of its weight. Important enzymes, such as invertase, which are added by bees, are needed to invert sugars into simpler forms of glucose and fructose. Glucose oxidase is another enzyme that forms hydrogen peroxide in honey, which subsequently helps prevent spoilage. There are small quantities of amino acids, and vitamins but make no mistake—honey is a super-saturated sugar solution that is desired for its sweetness.

Honey Fermentation. Honey will ferment under the right conditions. Sugar-tolerant yeasts chemically act on glucose and fructose to produce alcohol and carbon dioxide. If the moisture in the honey crop, measured with a hand refractometer, is less than 17.1%, the honey is safe from fermentation. However, if the moisture content is greater than 20%, the honey will be in constant danger of fermentation. Honey with moisture content of 18.6% is considered average and is reasonably safe from fermentation. Some cases of fermentation can be caused by granulated honey having higher moisture content near the top of the container.

Water Absorbing Nature of Honey. Due to its chemical configuration, honey has the characteristic of absorbing moisture from the air. However, honey's ability to absorb moisture from the air makes it a popular ingredient in baked goods. Cakes and breads made with honey stay moist longer than those made with other sugars.

Honey Granulation. Occasionally, some types of honey will granulate. Essentially some honeys have more sugar than they can hold in solution, and these excess sugars settle out or precipitate. Though there is a small risk of diluted honey near the surface of the jar fermenting, extracted honey in the granulated state is normal. It can be re-liquefied by loosening the jar lid and heating it in a water bath. The water should not boil (about 150° F maximum). Special heaters must be used to liquefy large amounts.

Figure 89. Honey that has begun to granulate.

Cooking With Honey

Under humid conditions, honey will absorb moisture from the air making it an excellent sweetener for baked goods and other recipes. To substitute honey in a recipe requiring sugar, reduce the amount of honey by about 1/4 cup. (i.e. one cup of sugar equals 3/4 cup of honey.) Adding 1/4 teaspoon of baking soda per cup of honey will help reduce the acidity in honey. Finally, since honey caramelizes at a lower temperature than sugar, reduce the oven temperature by about 25° F in order to prevent over-browning. Milder light-colored honeys (clover, fireweed, or alfalfa) are preferable for sweetening tea, coffee, or light baked goods. Strong-flavored honeys such as orange blossom, Ti-Ti, or sage are suitable for breakfast foods like pancakes or toast.

Figure 90. Bread made with honey and using creamed honey as a topping.

Figure 91. Three styles of honey dishes.

There is no denying that honey can be sticky to use and difficult to pour, but the reward will be worth the extra effort. Small amounts of honey can be held in drip-cut pitchers, like common small maple syrup pitchers. Honey can be warmed and will then flow much more like water. In fact, honey can be diluted with water. One-third cup of water per one cup of honey will roughly equal the consistency of maple syrup.

Honey has always been a premier sweetener. A varied assortment of honey dishes and servers are available. Indeed, cut-comb honey dishes are collectible antiques.

Honey Exhibits and Displays. Honey is frequently displayed at fairs, craft shows, or farm markets. Such exhibits vary in scope from a few entries to large and impressive displays. Honey shown at bee meetings or fairs may even be judged for quality and purity. Trained honey judges, of varying abilities, evaluate the entries and assign points. Entrants with the highest points are presented awards. The competent judge will use a refractometer, used to estimate the percentage of water present, and a polariscope, which is a lighted device having polarizing filters to detect cloudiness or other contaminants in the honey. Additionally, honey taste and visual presentation of the jar and lid will be evaluated.

Figure 92. A polariscope, refractometer and color grader.

Even so, choosing the best honey entry in a show can be difficult with only the slightest blemishes determining the winner. Fingerprints on jars or scratches on the jar lid are examples of small points that are used to separate winners from losers. In judged displays, other beekeeping commodities, such as wax and crafts, are also evaluated, but extracted honey is always the premier category at these shows.

Figure 93. A honey exhibit at a bee meeting.

Is Honey a Health Food? Yes, though honey is a healthy food, it should not be consumed excessively. Too much honey can result in excessive caloric intake. Diabetics should consult with their physician before eating honey. Though there are vitamins and enzymes in honey, they are only present in small amounts and do not satisfy minimum daily requirements. Honey should be eaten in moderation as a healthy sweetener.

Frequently, allergy sufferers report improvements in allergic responses to pollen allergies after eating local honey for a while. No doubt, some people are benefited, but in general, bees forage for heavy pollen that is intended to be collected by insects. Most allergy sufferers are responding to wind-blown pollens such as ragweed or grass. Bees do not usually collect these types of pollen.

Honey Production

Honey bees need honey as their only carbohydrate source. Pollen is the bees' only protein source. In the natural scheme of things, a natural bee nest would be much smaller than a managed hive, would swarm more often, and would produce less honey. As in all other aspects of agriculture, beekeepers and scientists have worked for many years to increase productivity of the managed hive.

Honey Production from Nectar. Foraging bees do not have small stainless steel buckets in which to gather nectar and pollen. The reality of honey elaboration is that bees must swallow the nectar to transport it back to the hive. Though some people may find this procedure a bit offensive, it is no more repulsive than a hen laying an egg or a steer being slaughtered.

The bee uses specialized mouthparts to form a structure similar to a soda straw. Nectar from a flower is sucked into the mouth, and passes through the esophagus. Nectar being collected for honey production for the hive never reaches the foraging bee's true stomach, but is gathered into an elastic structure called the honey sac (the crop). The crop is closed on both ends by valves that the forager bee can control. When full, the crop will hold less than a drop of nectar, but that drop may make up about 90% of the bee's weight. During the process of collecting nectar, and later when other house bees are storing and ripening nectar, the secretions of various glands, such as the salivary glands, hypopharyngeal glands, and mandibular glands are important in processing and ripening honey. Essentially, these glands change the sugars in nectar from complex to simple sugars that both bees and humans can readily digest.

Upon returning from the field, a forager bee will transfer her nectar load to a house bee for processing and storage. Nectar contains too much water to be stored. The house bee takes the drop of nectar she received and pumps it onto the bottom surface of her mouth where the moisture is partially evaporated. The nectar is drawn into the crop and then pumped out again. Taking about fifteen minutes, this cyclic process occurs several times, and results in honey that is about half-ripened. This is the active stage of moisture evaporation. House bees then spread the half-

Figure 94. A forager coming in for a landing.

ripened honey in empty cells, while other bees actively maintain high hive temperatures to evaporate moisture from the nectar (passive stage). This final ripening takes about 1–3 days. The reconstituted nectar has a different chemical configuration, with a lower moisture content of about 18.6% and is called honey.

Spring Management for the Honey Crop

The essentials of spring management and hive equipment are discussed elsewhere. They are important if the maximum honey crop is to be achieved. After the early bloom has passed and the primary honey plants are beginning to bloom, preparations for supering the colony should be made. Though there are two schools of thought on supering, the main point of both supering schemes is to have extra space on the colony in time for the bees to store and process nectar. Ideally, a strong colony, housed in two deep brood boxes, will need two to three supers. When they are filled with honey, the beekeeper may be required to extract the crop and put the supers on once again. Colonies can be stacked high with supers, but they become top heavy and can topple over on a windy day.

The top super should always be no more than half-full. If the inner cover is soundly stuck down with burr and brace comb, the beekeeper probably missed part of the honey crop due to inadequate space. At the beginning of the season, colonies should be given abundant space and supers should be added when the one already in place approaches half full. As the flow ends for the season, extra space should be limited, in order to force bees to finish capping partially processed honey and outer empty frames should be repositioned in the center of the super.

Figure 95. A full honey super.

A heavy nectar flow is an amazing experience. In just a few days, a powerful colony can store 40–60 pounds of honey including the construction of combs. Honey weighs about twelve pounds per gallon. Supers are heavy when full. When colonies are well prepared and the season is coming on strong, the beekeeper must be alert to intense short-term needs of the bees. Extra space can abruptly be in short supply.

Swarming is a normal problem during this time of the year. The colonies are increasing population and the incoming food supply is abundant. It is a good time for the bees to make a natural colony split. However, by swarming, the beekeeper will lose much of the honey crop that the colony would have produced. Providing space within the brood nest for honey storage and maintaining a young queen in the colony will help to limit swarms. However, swarming will never be eliminated.

Removing the Honey Crop

Frequently called "robbing the bees" by older beekeepers, taking surplus honey from the colonies is a normal aspect of beekeeping.

If a beekeeper is removing honey from only a few colonies (or from a few frames), the bees may simply be brushed from the combs with a stiff bristle brush. Brushes purchased from a bee supply operation or snowbrushes and other household brushes work well. Brushing bees from frames is time consuming and causes the bees to become defensive. Smoking the colony while brushing bees will make the task of removing surplus honey proceed more smoothly. After cold weather has set in, honey supers can frequently be removed with ease. That is assuming no bees are clustered within the supers. However, the honey must be warmed before it can be extracted.

A common way for a beekeeper to remove supers from a few colonies is to use the Porter Bee Escape. This small gadget fits within the handhold of an inner cover. An inner cover fitted with a bee escape is called an escape board. The escape board is placed under the full supers and the outer cover is repositioned on top of the colony. Bees in the supers file back down through the bee escape, which only allows bees to leave the supers as the evening cools. Bee escapes do not work well if the nighttime temperature does not drop enough for the bees to need to return to the brood nest area. Additionally, since bees cannot return to the supers, the beekeeper must watch for robbing activities through cracks within the super.

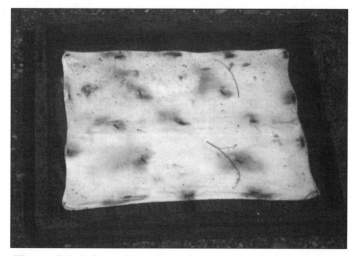

Figure 96. A fume board used to remove honey supers.

Chemical repellents are available from bee supply companies. Butyric anhydride is the basic component of one common repellent. Repellents are sprinkled on absorbent pads or thick cloth stapled to inner covers. Inner covers modified in this way or boards built specifically for this purpose are called fume boards. Depending on weather conditions, the chemical is sprinkled on the pads, placed on top of the colonies, and left there for a few minutes. In some parts of the United States, the backs of fume boards are painted black to adsorb heat that will aid the vaporization process. Pads should stay in place only long enough to start the bees moving downward. Puffing smoke into the colony first will help the repellent begin to work. Rarely, would more than two tablespoons (30 ml) of chemical be required per pad to start the process. Pads should be recharged when the bees are no longer responding to the fume boards. The repellent pads should not be left on the colonies any longer than necessary, and repellents should never be allowed to come in contact with honey. If bees begin to come out around the pad or out the front of the colony, too much repellent has been used or the pads have been left on too long. The beekeeper is advised to apply too little material, rather than too much.

Bee blowers are low pressure/high volume forced air devices. Bee supply companies sell such devices. Occasionally, the exhaust from shop vacuums will be great enough to blow bees from supers. However, the high pressure generated by air compressors is too great and can result in damaged bees. The blowing process is fast and relatively simple. The process does distribute the aroma of honey all over the yard, resulting in robbing behavior. The beekeeper should work quickly and keep all supers covered.

Figure 97. Using a bee blower to remove bees from supers.

No procedure for removing bees from supers is perfect. In fact, a combination of procedures will probably offer the best results. The bee-keepers should always expect a few bees to remain in the supers, regardless of the removal systems used.

Extracting and Processing the Honey Crop

The room selected for processing honey is a primary part of the small bee operation. A screened porch, an enclosed garage, a basement room, or the kitchen are all rooms that are commonly used by the small beekeeper as a honey processing center. Hot and cold water for clean-up and a well-lighted work area make the extracting process proceed smoothly.

Figure 98. A modern hobby extracting setup.

After removing the supers in the apiary, they should be covered and transported to the extracting area. Extracting should commence after taking the honey from the bees. Simple boards with rims, called drip boards, are useful in preventing leaking honey from dripping to the floor.

Basic Extracting Line Components:

1. An uncapping knife or uncapping device
2. An uncapping tank
3. An extractor
4. A sump or bucket
5. A filter (somewhat optional)
6. A settling tank
7. A bottling tank (somewhat optional).

The uncapping knife will cut cappings better if it is heated—either electrically or by hot water.

Figure 99. Hand-held uncapping tools.

The uncapping tank will need a bottom valve for honey to drain. This tank should be a comfortable height to manipulate heavy frames. Normally, waist-high is comfortable for most people. Stainless steel extractors can be expensive, but there are no easy substitutes for this device. As honey drains from the extractor, it needs to be caught in something. Electrically heated sumps with pumps are available from bee supply companies. Most hobby beekeepers simply use buckets, making certain that they do not overflow. Either the pump pushes the honey to the settling tank, or the beekeeper pours honey from the extractor bucket into the settling tank. If allowed to sit for a few days, honey in a settling tank has time for bubbles, the occasional bee body part, wax, or propolis to rise to the top where it can be skimmed off. Honey can be bottled straight from the settling tank, but a final filtering into a bottling tank assures the beekeeper that the honey has been filtered well. Being a stable food product, once the honey has been extracted, it can be stored in covered plastic buckets for years if specific storage conditions are met. Honey should be stored at 50° F or lower. Actually, storing below freezing is not a bad idea. Storage between 50° F and 59° F, encourages granulation. Temperatures around 81° F can rapidly damage flavor, color and enzyme content.

Commercial Honey Processing Equipment. Commercial honey processing equipment is similar to hobby processing equipment, except larger in every regard. Due to the weight of honey, various kinds

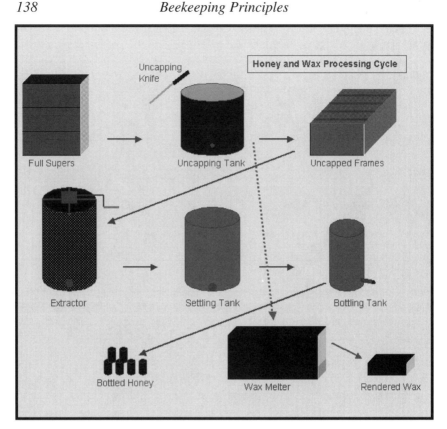

Figure 100. A generalized honey and wax processing sequence for the beginner.

of lifts and loaders are used. Also the heavy weight requires sound floors that can stand constant cleaning and heavy wear. An area of greater mechanization is in honey filtering. Letting tons of honey sit in settling tanks for several days is not practical, so honey is flash-heated and filtered before being bottled or stored.

A beekeeper normally decides to become full-time after a long period of experience and practice. Estimates are risky, but in general, about 400 colonies are all that one healthy person can maintain. As the operation grows to maintain several thousand, the operation must become more mechanized or more employees must be added to provide the needed labor.

The commercial market for the honey is critical. Generally, commercial honey-producing operations grow in numbers as their customers' demand for honey grows.

A commercial bee operation must have the following attributes: (1) a market for the honey crop, (2) bee yard locations, (3) mechanical expertise in woodworking, machinery maintenance, and electrical principles, (4) business experience, and (5) legal and regulatory expertise (i.e. taxes, liability, interstate regulations).

Figure 101. A commercial honey bottling operation.

Producing Comb Honey

In the early years of beekeeping, honey was not extracted, but was eaten in the comb. Many honey purists insist that the best flavor of honey is achieved from comb honey. Certainly, the extracting process is an ideal time for delicate volatiles to be lost as the extractor exposes the combs and honey to air.

Since little processing equipment is required, comb honey is easier to process than extracted honey. Honeycomb can be cut from the frame and is called "cut-comb" honey. Honey produced in special boxes or plastic circles is called "section honey" or "rounds." If a piece of cut comb is placed in a jar having all extra space filled with liquid honey, the product is call "chunk honey." It has always been popular in the Southeastern United States.

Though little processing equipment is required and comb honey tends to have a better flavor, it is not always easy to produce. Frequently bees

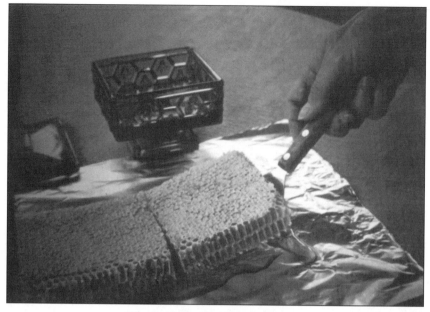

Figure 102. Cut comb honey.

will not readily work specialty supers and will either swarm or simply shut down. The essence of comb honey production are: (1) maintain a strong colony, (2) head the colony with a young queen to inhibit it swarming, (3) do not mix other types of supers with the specialty honey supers and (4) hope for a strong nectar flow. A large swarm can be used to produce copious amounts of comb honey. Bees from a large swarm are in a honey-producing frame of mind. They have already swarmed so their swarming tendency is low, however, getting a large swarm is never guaranteed.

Section Comb Honey Equipment

Section comb honey is generally produced in 4-1/2" x 4-1/4" basswood section boxes. Specially modified supers are required to hold the sections while the bees are filling them. Alternatively, plastic round equipment (Ross Rounds) has been developed that requires little assembly. In both types of equipment, the management procedure is the same.

Though comb honey is pretty and tasteful, partially filled combs have limited value. Many times, the best sections are sold, while the partially filled sections are the ones that the beekeeper eats.

Eating Comb Honey

When frames are prepared with foundation, only thin foundation free from plastic and wires and intended for human consumption is used.

Figure 103. Full Ross Round™ honey frames.

Special honey dishes are available both as current housewares and as antiques to grace a formal table. Comb honey is cut from the chunk and is eaten just as jam or fruit preserves are eaten. Humans are not able to metabolize the wax, but no digestive harm is done.

Creamed Honey Production

Creamed honey is finely granulated honey. Actually, most types of honey will granulate and form a crude type of creamed honey, but this product is usually gritty tasting. A good creamed honey product should have the texture of butter. The lightest, mildest flavored honey makes the best creamed honey, but darker, fuller flavored honeys will also make acceptable creamed honey.

The four important elements in making creamed honey are: heating, straining, mixing, and cooling. Honey for creaming should be in the moisture range of 17.5%–18.0%. The honey is heated to 150° F to destroy all the yeast present and to dissolve any coarse glucose crystals. The hot honey is strained through fine filters to remove any remaining contaminants. Cool the honey to room temperature as quickly as possible. At this point "starter" seed is added to the cool honey (about 5–10% by weight). The easiest place to get starter crystals is from another creamed honey product. Otherwise, making finely ground crystals for granulation can be labor-intensive, requiring specialized grinders. Be certain that the honey is no hotter than 75° F when the starter seed is added, or the starter seed may dissolve. The honey containing the starter seed must be thoroughly mixed. Commercial producers have large tanks with horizontal mixers. Try not to include too much air, since bubbles will rise to the surface causing a scum appearance.

Marketing the Honey Crop

Too often beekeepers are too good at producing honey, but not particularly good at selling it. As one way of disposing of the crop, hobby beekeepers are notorious for producing honey and giving it away. That is not a problem, so long as that particular individual is not interested in making any money from the honey crop.

Honey can be sold at two major levels, locally as a specialty crop and broadly to any available market. Selling honey locally as a specialty crop is much easier than any other marketing method. Additionally, it probably generates the most income from the crop.

Selling Honey Locally

Honey produced in the area in which it is sold, is always in demand and normally sells easily. Local honey has been successfully sold at county fairs, flea markets, roadside markets, from the home of the beekeeper, and from small commercial markets. At all times, the bottled honey must be immaculately clean, both inside and outside the jar.

Cleanliness. Though beekeepers are perfectly aware that bees produce the honey, the unenlightened consumer would be horrified to find a

Figure 104. Selling honey at a flea market.

bee in the honey. Even if the crop is small and only a few jars are sold, keep the processing area clean. Consider wearing a hair net. One cannot be too careful when selling honey products to the public.

Selling Location. Many hobby beekeepers sell honey from their homes. This is both convenient and inconvenient. The beekeeper is away either when the customer stops by or is busy with something else when the call comes. Alternatively, the entire inventory is handy and no rent is paid on a commercial booth or other sales space.

Labeling. In the past, homemade labels were crude, but with today's computer software programs, clever, professional looking labels can be created. If the beekeeper does not have computer equipment or the necessary skill, going to a commercial "quick print" shop for assistance is a consideration. Of course, bee supply companies make ready-made labels. Use a label that does not show an actual bee but pictures honey, food, or flowers. Too often, the public does not like any bugs, even if they are honey bees.

Figure 105. A honey jar label.

Pricing the Product. There is no easy procedure for determining the selling price of the product. There are innumerable business procedures for determining costs but for most hobby beekeepers, such advanced procedures are not necessary. The National Honey Board[11] is a

---

[11]National Honey Board, 390 Lashley Street, Longmont, CO 80501-6045 / (800) 553-7162 / www.nhb.org / www.honey.com

helpful source of information on all aspects of honey including pricing information. It is suggested to visit several markets to determine the selling price for commercial honey. Do not sell hard-earned honey for too little. Normally, locally produced honey brings a higher price than commercially packed honey. Though advertising is always helpful, it is rarely practical for the small hobby producer.

Commercial Markets for Honey. The selling price is considerably lower, but honey can be sold to commercial honey packers at wholesale prices. Not as much money is earned, but the requirements for marketing are practically eliminated. Beekeepers with enough hives to begin to accumulate unsold honey may sell honey both ways, locally and commercially.

CHAPTER 24
The Two-Queen System for Maximum Honey Production

The Two-Queen System is a well-documented, though complex, procedure for using the offspring from two queens to build up a colony quickly. The concepts in this book are directed primarily at the novice beekeeper, making the discussion of this complicated two-queen procedure somewhat out-of-place. Even so, it can be performed by a beekeeper with limited experience. Although two queens are used to buildup the colony, only one queen remains after the procedure is completed.

The Procedure[12]. The basic technique is to make an early split from a strong colony, probably about the time of fruit bloom. Add a new queen to the split. The best time for making the colony split is about two months before the primary nectar flow begins. Build the colony up during early spring by stimulatory feeding—both pollen substitute and sugar syrup. The adult bee population going into the flow should be considerably greater than the adult bee population from one colony alone.

Procedure for Establishing Two-Queen Colonies for Honey Production:

1. Divide a strong over-wintered colony into halves and provide a new queen to the queenless part. Feed both halves with pollen substitute and sugar syrup.
2. Place most of the unsealed brood with the old queen and sealed brood with the new queen and divide the adult bees evenly between the two splits.
3. Place the box with the old queen on the bottom board.
4. Add an empty brood chamber with an inner cover (close the hand hold) or a screen divider on top. At this point, the colony halves are completely separated.
5. Place the box with the new queen on top of the inner cover or screen divider and provide that with an entrance.
6. In about two weeks, replace the inner cover or screen divider with a queen excluder and add an empty brood chamber to the top half of the hive.
7. It may be necessary to perform several brood chamber reversals in their respective halves to promote faster build-up and control swarming. This might have to be done every week until 20 to 30 days before the end of the major nectar flow.

---

[12]Adapted from the procedure of B. Furgala, University Of Minnesota.

8. Honey supers may have to be added to the upper and lower units as needed.
9. At about 20 to 30 days before the end of the major flow go into the bottom half of the hive and dispose of the old queen. Put the hive back together leaving the queen excluder off.
10. Full honey supers can be removed at any time during the process.

Normal overwintered colony

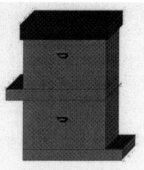

Divide and give each half a queen

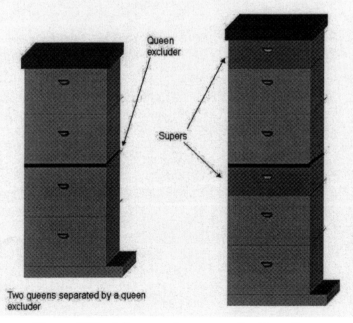

Queen excluder

Supers

Two queens separated by a queen excluder

Figure 106. A 2-queen honey production plan.

Advantages

The advantages to the Two-Queen System are that it will equalize the population of all colonies and use less equipment to produce more honey. Swarming and supersedure are usually lower because of the introduction of new queens and the way the system is managed. Such hives generally winter better.

Disadvantages

This system will require a large amount of labor in manipulating and managing the system. The beekeeper must stay on schedule. Because of the high volume of honey produced, the hives become tall and tip easily. Tipping can be avoided if supers are removed as soon as they are filled. The Two-Queen System only works where there are long major nectar flows.

Variations on the Method

Occasionally, beekeepers will only super the top of the colony thereby avoiding removing the two deeps to get to the lower colony. Secondly, beekeepers may simply break the system down to one queen as the nectar flow develops. Keep in mind that any eggs laid much beyond the middle of the flow will be of no use as nectar foragers.

CHAPTER 25

Nectar and Pollen Sources for Honey Bees

Honey bee foragers are opportunist and will forage on the food source that yields the greatest reward. Beekeepers frequently want to plant food sources for their colonies. However, the beekeeper or gardener should know that bees will forage far from their home hive. In many cases, over approximately 18,000 A. Therefore, providing small plantings are mainly for the enjoyment of watching bees forage within the garden. Though honey bees will readily work such small plantings, when considered alone, they generally offer minimal rewards.

Major Sources of Nectar and Pollen. Major sources of food for honey bees vary widely across the USA. In general, clovers are a universal nectar and pollen source. Other common regional sources are Basswood, Tulip Poplar and Goldenrod. However, most major sources are regionalized and found only in distinct areas. Examples of major nectar sources that are not widely distributed are: Orange, Almond, and Fireweed. By definition, a major source will have to be abundantly common.

Figure 107. Tulip poplar, a primary nectar source in many areas.

Minor Sources of Nectar and Pollen. Opposite to major sources, minor sources are frequently inconspicuous even approaching invisibility. However, minor sources, when combined, easily equal the value of the more glamorous and showy major sources. As a group, they should be considered significant contributors to the hive's food stores. Minor sources also serve to provide additional nutritional needs to the colony not provided by the major sources.

Figure 108. Ornamental flowers, a common minor nectar source.

The significance of minor sources varies widely. In fact, during some years, minor sources may even exceed the output of the more commonly accepted major sources. Alternatively, minor sources may be such erratic producers as to be generally useless to the hive except during the odd year. There are thousands of plant species that contribute something, to the hive's food stores. To confuse the issue even more, a particular minor plant species may be productive in one area while being non-productive in another. For the immediate future, the usefulness of minor plant species as nectar and pollen producers to beehives will remain in the domain of anecdotal accounts offered by beekeepers. No doubt, honey crops are occasionally attributed to a specific minor source when it is actually produced by another.

Plants useful to bees as food sources. Beekeepers, gardeners, and growers frequently want to establish plantings to augment the bees' needs. To assist with that desire, an incomplete list is presented in Appendix 1, Pollen and Nectar Sources. Within the list, plants considered major producers are designated as such, but be aware that major nectar producers are not significant in all regions of the USA. The list of minor plants is incomplete. Such a list of minor sources would list thousands of plants. Consequently, minor plants of established importance have been included, but be alert for sources important in your area.

Additionally, many fruit and vegetable plants are not on the list that possibly should be. Common garden vegetables benefit from insect pollination, except for most varieties of peppers, tomatoes, and potatoes. Within the list, no effort is made to indicate whether a plant is considered a weed, a hybrid, or an exotic plant. Use the list as an aid, but not necessarily the final tool for decision-making when selecting nectar and pollen producing plants.

CHAPTER 26

Pollen and Pollination

Within the bee world, pollination has historically been the little brother of honey production. However, during recent years, due in large part to the predatory activities of Varroa mites, the perception of honey bees as dependable pollinators has increased significantly among both beekeepers and the public.

Within any pollination scheme, there must be a 4-way agreement between the beekeeper, the grower, the bees, and the flowering plants. Beekeepers charge colony rental fees, growers sell the fruit or vegetables produced, bees get pollen and nectar for their food use, and plants set fruit containing seeds for their next generation. Obviously, within such a complex agreement, there is a lot of room for wobble. The weather is the biggest variable about which none of the four parties can control. It affects everything during the pollination season. Too cold, too dry, too warm, too wet, too windy and the four components' objectives are made more difficult. Ironically, all human involvement can evaporate and the relationship between plants and pollinating insects is the same.

The Relationship between Flowering Plants and Pollinating Insects. It is unclear how the close relationship between plants and their pollinators developed, but the relationship is well established now. Flowering plants need insect vectors to move pollen from one blossom to another, while pollinating insects need pollen and nectar as a food source.

Figure 109. A honey bee pollen collector on dandelion.

It is physiologically expensive for plants to produce excess pollen and nectar. Different plants employ different strategies to attract insect foragers to mature blossoms. Some plants will offer high levels of sugar concentration in the nectar, but may not offer as many amino acids within the pollen. Other plants may offer no nectar at all, but will offer high quality pollen. Yet, others may offer their food resources at early or late times within the foraging season. In essence, plants must compete for the services that insect pollinators provide.

Honey bee foragers must meet two types of needs, immediate and future. To meet immediate needs, foragers will frequently take the first flower types to be found—regardless of quality. In a pollen-stressed hive during early spring, it is as though the hive has thousands of hungry, crying baby bees at home that are all needing to be fed. After that initial need is met, foragers can spend more time searching for richer food sources and will begin to follow the progress of the season in storing pollen and nectar for the next winter. The various strategies used by both flowering plants and foraging bees are complex. Simply putting bee hives within a crop planting offering low quality rewards will not insure that foragers will stay on the targeted blossoms. Successful foragers will "shop around" for better food sources, just as people do within a supermarket.

The Pollination Procedure. Basic pollination is the transfer of pollen from the stamens (male component) to the pistil (female component) of flowers. To a degree, such flowers are said to be cross-pollinated. For example, cucumber plants produce both male and female blossoms. Insects must move pollen from the male blossom to the female

General Pollination Schemes

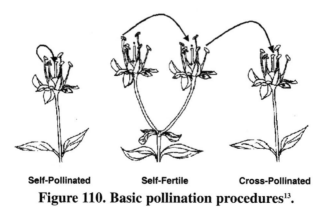

Self-Pollinated   Self-Fertile   Cross-Pollinated

Figure 110. Basic pollination procedures[13].

---

[13]Schematic modified from *Bee Pollination of Crops in Ohio,* Ohio State University Extension, Bulletin 559

blossom for a cucumber to develop. Each seed within the cucumber fruit represents a transferred pollen grain. Other plants will self-pollinate or pollen grains from a specific flower will fertilize the ovules of the same flower. It is possible for a particular plant to be able to self-pollinate, but to show increased yields if insect pollination (cross-pollination) is provided. For cross-pollination to occur, the plants must be compatible. The three pathways presented in the figure are generalizations. Pollination requirements for specific plants vary widely.

Insects are not the only vectors of pollen. Other plants may use birds, wind, water, and even bats to move pollen from one blossom to another. Generally, plants pollinated by birds have deep flowers while plants employing wind as the pollen transfer agent have plain blossoms. Pines are examples of plants using wind. Catkins on pines during spring months are common, but they are not colorful. There is no need for colorful petals since insects or other animals are not being attracted. Honey bees will frequently work wind-pollinated plants for pollen sources. Foraging bee activity does not noticeably increase yields from these plants. It is ironic that the pretty blossoms that humans enjoy for their aesthetic qualities are for bees.

The Bee Forager's Pollen Collection Procedure. All honey bees are covered in plumose or branched body hair. When on pollen producing flowers, their fuzzy bodies quickly become covered by pollen grains. Commonly a bee will hover near a blossom it has just completed servicing and will groom itself. Grooming (pollen accumulation) is accomplished by the bee regurgitating a small amount of nectar and wetting herself with it. Then, using combs on her legs, she accumulates the

Figure 111. Pollen pellets in a pollen trap.

pollen grains into clumps. These small clumps are passed to the rear legs where they are packed together within the corbicula or pollen basket. The accumulated clumps are compressed and formed into pollen pellets made up of thousand of pollen grains and a small amount of nectar—all reinforced with a few strategic hairs.

Upon returning to the hive, the forager finds an appropriate cell, hangs by her front legs, and scrapes the pellets off into the cell. Later, a house bee spies the freshly-collected pellets and she, too, adds nectar/honey to the pellets and compresses them tightly into the cell. Several loads are required to fill the cell. Such pollen stored in cells, near the brood nest, is called "Bee Bread." Due to the digestive effects of the enzymes in the nectar and honey that is mixed into the pollen pellets, the pollen is no longer viable as a pollination agent. It is partially digested in preparation for nurse bees feeding on it.

Beekeepers as Commercial Pollinators

Humans have significantly altered the ecology across the USA from what it was when this country was considered new. For example, on Maryland's eastern shore, lima bean fields covering hundreds of acres are common. Giant almond orchards in California have replaced natural vegetation and with it have gone natural nesting sites for native pollinators. Consequently, such large acreages oftentimes do not have enough pollinators to effectively pollinate such a large monoculture block. For many years now, commercial beekeepers have temporarily relocated bee colonies into such commercial plantings as apples, almonds, blueberries, and melons.

Figure 112. Rental hives in a commercial apple orchard.

Growers are on a tight production schedule and want bee colonies in place at just the right time for blossom pollination. Just as quickly, they will want the colonies removed as the petals begin to drop, in order for them to continue with disease control programs. Beekeepers and growers both need to be understanding and professional during this time. Growers should not apply insecticides while the bees are in the orchard. Beekeepers should be aware of the stress of fruit and vegetable production. A written pollination agreement is useful in avoiding future problems.

Pollination Contracts. Written agreements can range from simple documents with appropriate signatures to sophisticated legal documents.

Major points normally covered within the Pollination contract are:

1. Date of the document
2. Names of both the beekeeper and the grower
3. Location of the orchards or fields
4. Approximate date that the colonies will be needed
5. Number of colonies and their composition
6. Rental price of the colonies
7. Where the colonies will be set off
8. Dates that the colonies should be in and out of the orchard
9. Grower agrees not to spray insecticides while the colonies are on location

In more advanced contracts, other points such as payment for under-strength colonies, accessibility for hive management, and whether or not the colonies are to be moved while on location are other considerations that can be discussed. Many times, only a handshake and a verbal agreement are enough to get the deal done. There is much to be said for dependability from both parties. Even so, a written agreement is much better. What if the orchard owner dies or goes bankrupt while the bees are on location? What if the beekeeper suffers serious illness or suffers a mechanical breakdown? What if a stinging incident occurs while the bees are on location? The general written contract is more important for a doomsday document than an simple operational agreement.

Pollen Trapping. Pollen for uses other than those that are bee-related have not been historically significant in the United States. The primary use for pollen is still as a component of pollen substitute. Apparently, the aromas and tastes of collected pollen can be used to enhance the attractiveness of pollen substitutes that are commercially produced or are home-produced.

Pollen Trap Designs. Commercial vendors offer pollen traps for sale within catalogs. In recent years, the number and diversity of traps for sale have declined. Even so several models are still available. Building pollen traps in the shop is possible.

Broadly described, there are two types of pollen traps, those that are beneath the bottom brood chamber and models that are mounted on the front of colony. The heart of any trap is a grid through which pollen-loaded bees can squeeze themselves, but not the accompanying pollen loads. Holes bored to the diameter of 5/16" or 5-mesh galvanized hardware cloth are the two openings that can be used to make the grids. The five-mesh hardware cloth is not commonly available in hardware stores but can be obtained from bee supply sources.

Figure 113. A modern pollen trap.

Several things happen to the colony from which pollen is being trapped. First, as expected, the colony will become pollen-deprived and will suffer nutritionally if the trap is left in place too long. Some trap designs allow the trap to stay in place but allows the grid mechanism to be removed. Though difficult to make global recommendations, collecting pollen for about three days and then giving one–two days off does not seem to harm the colony. Another characteristic of most pollen traps is that they confine drones within the colony. Frequently, drones become stuck in the grid requiring the occasional clearing of the screen grid. Finally, the pollen trap models that require the common entrance to be moved will cause temporary entrance confusion. After about a day, that will be resolved.

Collected pollen should be cleaned, probably by hand, and frozen in small quantities. Pollen is bacterially active. When frozen in quantities as small as a few gallons, bacterial activity within the center of the pollen mass can form a "hot spot" and will allow the pollen to spoil. An alternative is permanent freezing to dry the pollen until it is hard and brittle. Simple drying devices such as a goose-neck lamp with a 100-watt incandescent bulb can be used to dry a shallow layer of freshly collected pollen. Obviously, various types of ovens can also be used, but do not overheat the pollen. After drying, the pollen should be frozen to be certain that all wax moth eggs have been killed. At that point, either hold the pollen in the frozen state or move it to tightly closed containers held at room temperature.

Feeding Pollen Substitutes to Colonies

Bee bread (stored pollen) does not hold up nutritionally for much more than a year and is rarely seen in large amounts in late winter. Pollen substitutes are frequently fed to late-wintering colonies in order for them build up earlier and stronger. Though this is a great attribute for the colony coming out of winter, it should be known that such a strong colony is likely to swarm later in the spring. Therefore, successfully feeding a pollen substitute will result in a populous colony that will require swarm prevention later in the year.

Pollen substitutes should be put on the colony before any naturally occurring pollen becomes available. For most beekeepers, this will be in late winter. The substitute should go on the top bars as near to the cluster as possible. Any substitute not consumed by the time spring has arrived should be discarded.

If ready-made substitutes are not purchased, there are a number of home recipes. The mixes will make a dry powder or a moist patty. Bees eat both reasonably well. As with sugar syrup, some colonies will consume

Figure 114. Dry pollen substitute being fed to colonies in the early spring.

the pollen substitute better than others will. There is nothing to be done about this.

Recipes For Pollen Supplement Mixes

Soybean Flour Mix (Moist Mix)

1. One pound of bee pollen
2. Three pounds of soybean flour
3. Five and one-third pounds of granulated sugar
4. Two and two-thirds pounds of water

This recipe will make twelve pounds of pollen supplement.

Soybean Flour Mix (Moist Mix) (Small Portion)

1. 2 oz pollen
2. 6 oz of soybean flour
3. 5-1/2 oz water
4. 10-1/2 oz granulated sugar

This recipe makes one pollen supplement cake.

Soybean Flour Dry Mix

1. Three parts soybean flour
2. One part pollen

This recipe should be fed in an open sheltered container.

Brewer's Yeast Mix (Moist Mix)

1. One pound of pollen
2. Three pounds of brewer's yeast
3. Seven pounds of sugar
4. One pound of water

This recipe will make twelve pounds of pollen supplement.

The Nutritional Value of Pollen

Though not always the perfect food, pollen is highly nutritious. Most pollens are high in protein, vitamins, minerals and trace elements. The instinct of the colony's foragers is to collect from several sources at once, thereby minimizing the shortage that any one pollen type may have.

Pollen as a Human Food. Frequently, bee pollen is touted as a perfect food for humans. In fact, it is an excellent food, but not perfect and not without precautions. A common concern is that pollen will incite allergic responses from the person who eats it. In fact, there are few occasions that this has been shown. More common are digestive problems or stomach cramps. Bee-collected pollen has protein levels nearly as great as that of sirloin steak and surpasses nearly all other foods in vitamins and nutrient content.

CHAPTER 27

Recognizing and Treating the Bee Hive for Common Diseases and Pests

Honey bees have problems with pests and diseases. Honey bees hoard large amounts of concentrated carbohydrates and protein. They live in cramped, moist, quarters and in perpetuity. It is a great environment for a pest or pathogen.

Obviously, if bees lost every battle with its specialized pestilence, there would long since have been no bees. Obviously, bees do have defensive measures that work reasonably well. Though predacious mites have taken a great toll, honey bees are still in relative abundance. Judicious help from the beekeeper can go a long way in helping bees in their battles against some diseases and pests.

Broadly speaking, honey bees are affected by parasitic mites, bacterial diseases, fungal diseases, viruses, protozoa, and a host of predators such as wax moths, bears, and beetles. Other than possibly requeening, the beekeeper can discard from the list viruses and fungal diseases as problems with which the beekeeper can do little to assist. There are simply no adequate controls for these maladies within beekeeping at this time. That leaves bacteria, protozoa, mites, and other pests such as bears, skunks, toads, or birds. Though all threats to the colony's good health should be addressed, the most common problems, American foulbrood and predacious mites (Varroa and Tracheal mites) should be given the most consideration by the beekeeper. The recent introduction of the Small Hive Beetle (*Aethina tumida*) has caused concern among beekeepers. Its true potential for damage is not yet known.

Treatment for honey bee diseases and pests. Treating bee colonies for various pathogenic problems can be both helpful and potentially harmful to the hive population and to the future honey crop. There are many variables that must be considered when developing broad scientific recommendations for disease and pest control. Those considerations must be reviewed over a period of years and under different environmental conditions. It is not a quick procedure. In most cases, for statistical analysis to be relevant, untreated hives must actually be allowed to die to conclusively show that a treatment is effective within the treated population. Beekeepers should be warned that looking for serendipitous treatments that are poorly researched is a risky procedure for the beekeeper, the bees, and the honey crop. Even if recommended and approved treatments seem to be increasingly ineffective, a beekeeper is wise to stick with tested and documented control procedures.

BACTERIAL AND OTHER PATHOGENIC DISEASES

American Foulbrood

Description and Spread. American foulbrood, or AFB, is caused by the bacterium *Paenibacillus (Bacillus) larvae*[14]. AFB has plagued both bees and beekeepers from the earliest days of United States beekeeping. *Paenibacillus (Bacillus) larvae* is a spore-forming bacterium. Spores are extremely hardy and can survive in dormancy for thirty-five years or more. Either infested bees or infected equipment easily transport spores. Beekeepers moving contaminated equipment are, by far, the greatest source of AFB spread.

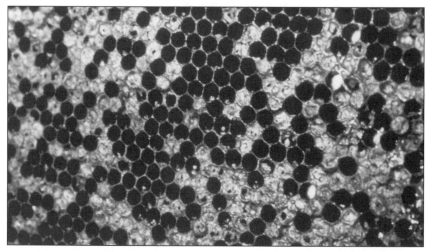

Figure 115. A brood frame infected with American foulbrood.

Symptoms. Visual signs of AFB begin to show up in the hive after young susceptible larvae eat the spores that have been mixed in the brood food fed by nurse bees. If left untreated, infection spreads rapidly until the colony population dies either from cold months or from wax moth attacks.

Symptoms of American Foulbrood:

1. Brown, decaying prepupa or early pupal stages
2. Spotty brood patterns
3. Punctured, ragged cappings
4. Musty decay odor (somewhat like sour, wet boots)

---

[14]*Bacillus larvae* was recently changed to *Paenibacillus larvae* subsp. *larvae*

Symptoms of American Foulbrood that are Occasionally Present:

1. Dead brood with the tongue sticking up from the carcass
2. Mucilaginous consistency of some pupae that will string out about an inch when punctured
3. Dried pupal skins, in the form of a brittle scale, stick to the bottom sides of infected cells (difficult to see)

Treatment. Burning infected equipment and destroying infected bees is the only way to completely eradicate AFB. Though effective, total colony destruction is a radical recommendation. Presently, oxytetracycline hydrochloride (Terramycin®) is the only approved antibiotic for controlling the growth and development of the bacteria, *Paenibacillus (Bacillus) larvae*, within the gut of the larvae. It does NOT kill spores; therefore, the disease will re-express itself shortly after antibiotic applications are stopped.

Figure 116. Terramycin being applied to a colony.

Treatment Doses. Stop all antibiotic treatments 4 weeks before the nectar flow starts. It is important to confirm dose recommendations with the state apiarist. Dose rates and recommendations vary from state to state.

1. Terramycin/Powdered Sugar Mixture: Mix one 6.4-oz package of TM25 with 1.5–2.0 pounds of powdered sugar. Dust outer edges of the brood frames. Usually, three dustings at 4-5 day intervals are considered one treatment per hive. Stop all treatments four weeks before supers are added.

2. Antibiotic Extender Patty: Mix 1/3 pound of vegetable shortening (e.g. Crisco) with 2/3 pound granulated sugar. Add two tablespoons of

TM25 to the mixture. Press into a 1/2 pound patty and place on the top bars of the brood frames. Do not leave on during a nectar flow. This procedure is not universally recommended.

Figure 117. Burning equipment that was heavily infected with American foulbrood.

When to Treat. Early spring before supers are put on. Actually, treatments can occur any time that surplus honey is not being produced.

European Foulbrood

Description and Spread. Essentially, European foulbrood (EFB) is the little brother of American foulbrood. Another bacterium, *Melissococcus pluton* (formerly *Streptococcus pluton*), is credited with causing the symptoms associated with EFB, though other bacteria probably play a role. The major difference between the two brood diseases is that EFB does NOT produce spores. Therefore, its persistence and effect on honey bees is greatly reduced when compared to AFB. Ironically, not much is known about EFB. No doubt, both drifting bees and beekeepers spread it. EFB attacks colonies in mid to late spring and has been called a stress disease. EFB is not usually considered serious, but since it resembles AFB, it should be treated with care.

Symptoms. Infected larvae usually die in the coiled larval "C" shape while larvae infected with AFB die stretched out. Initially larvae are yellow before changing to brown and finally to black.

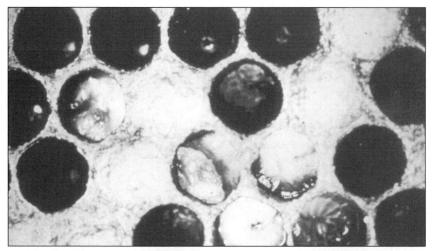

Figure 118. Larvae dying from European foulbrood.

Symptoms of European Foulbrood:

1. Spotty brood pattern
2. Twisted yellow-colored larvae
3. Sour, somewhat putrefied odor
4. Larva dries to a rubbery scale
5. Watery body fluids

Symptoms of European Foulbrood that are Occasionally Present:

1. Larvae dying in the extended position
2. Mucilaginous stringiness usually less than one inch

Treatment and Treatment Doses. Treatment is the same as for AFB and on the same time frame.

When to Treat. Treatment should occur in late winter or early spring before the nectar flow starts.

Nosema Disease

Description and Spread. The protozoan, *Nosema apis*, causes Nosema. Nosema infections have been compared to high-blood pressure in humans. It may be within a colony's population for years but may not express any symptoms. Cool, wet spring seasons seem to aggravate the development of latent Nosema. Beekeeper manipulations and robbing or drifting bees are the primary means of the spread of Nosema. *Nosema apis* is a spore-forming protozoan.

Symptoms. Extreme fecal markings on the hive's exterior are a common indicator of Nosema. However all dysentery infections are not due to Nosema. Bees with swollen abdomens and unhooked wings, crawling in front of a fecal-spotted hive are general indicators of Nosema, though those symptoms could also indicate other non-related problems. Internal examination of the infected bee would be required to tell if Nosema is the causative agent.

Figure 119. Fecal streaking on the hive exterior caused by Nosema.

Treatment. The antibiotic Fumidil-B® (fumagillin) gives excellent control of Nosema. Fumidil-B® should be mixed in cool sugar syrup at label rates.

When to Treat. Feed in the fall giving the colony enough time to incorporate the sugar syrup into the winter honey stores. A spring feeding may also help suppress Nosema, but should be stopped 4 weeks before the nectar flow starts if supers are to be added.

Other Commonly Occurring Diseases

Unfortunately, other diseases commonly occur, for which there is no control. Currently, no chemical controls are available for the viruses causing sacbrood and bee paralysis. Also, the common fungal disease, chalkbrood, has no chemical control.

MITE PESTS OF HONEY BEES

Varroa Mites

Description and Spread. The arrival and establishment of Varroa mites (*Varroa destructor*) in North America is now historical

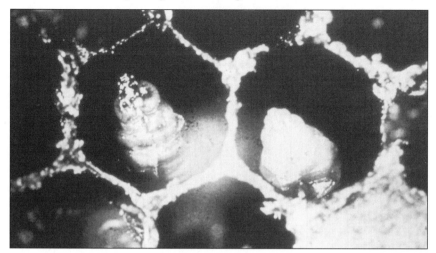

Figure 120. Sacbrood infected larvae.

fact. Within the continental USA, there are no areas considered Varroa mite-free. Originally, the mite was a parasite on *Apis cerana*, the Asian honey bee. By inadvertent beekeeper spread, the mite is presently found throughout the world except for Australia, and Hawaii. Its first arrival in the USA was in 1987. Varroa is a large tortoise-shaped mite that is colored rusty-red. The mite is a bit less that 1/16" across and is easily visible with the unaided eye.

Symptoms. Initially, the presence of Varroa is unnoticeable in the hive. Several months to several years may be required for mite populations to build up enough for them to be easily seen. By that time, both the adult and brood population are heavily infested and colony's death can occur rapidly. Dying colonies with abundant honey stores are a strong clue that Varroa mites were present in high numbers. Wingless or deformed bees that are either dead or maimed are also symptomatic of Varroa infestations. In such cases, mites can usually be found under the cappings enclosing larvae. Beekeepers within the United

Figure 121. A Varroa mite.

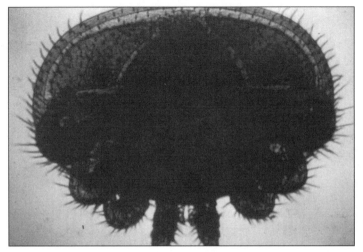

Figure 122. A ventral view of a Varroa mite showing its specialized legs.

States should assume that Varroa mites are present within their colonies. Approved treatments should be initiated on a regular basis.

　　Treatment. Use one Apistan® strip (active ingredient—fluvalinate) for each five combs of bees or less in each brood chamber. Hang strips within two combs of the edge of the bee cluster. Apistan® strips must be in contact with brood nest bees at all times. For best results, use strips when daytime temperatures are at least 50ºF. Presently, there are no other legal treatment materials for Varroa.

Figure 123. An Apistan® strip partially in place. A grease patty, used to control tracheal mites, is near the rear of the hive.

When to Treat. Treat in the spring before honey supers are put on and in the fall after supers have been taken off. Leave strips in place 42–56 days (6–8 weeks).

Tracheal Mites

Description and Spread. Tracheal mites (*Acarapis woodi*) are microscopic and live within the honey bee's respiratory system (predominately the prothoracic spiracle). They were first described in England in 1919 and not found in the USA until 1985. Research and development of information concerning the effects of tracheal mites have been given secondary status while control stratagems for Varroa have been developed. There are differing opinions as to how much of a threat tracheal mites are to USA beekeepers, especially for those who keep bees in warm climates.

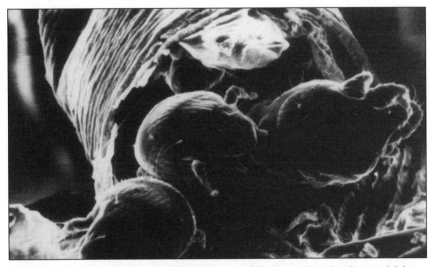

Figure 124. An electron scan of three adult tracheal mites within a worker bee's respiratory system.

Symptoms. Infected colonies have dwindling populations, do not cluster well, and often die in the winter (February and March), leaving behind large amounts of honey. Infested adults may act irritated or disoriented. Weak adults may be found crawling aimlessly near the hive entrance. Microscopic examination of the bees' respiratory system is required to show the presence of the tracheal mite. Authorities disagree as to the seriousness of the effects of tracheal mites on honey bees. Simply finding tracheal mites within the dissected bee does not always mean that disease symptoms will be expressed within the colony.

Treatment. Two materials, vegetable oil patties (Grease Patties) and menthol, are useful in suppressing tracheal mite populations.

(1) Vegetable shortening patties. Mix oil and sugar in a 1:2 ratio. The patty should be about the size of a hamburger patty (about 1/4 pound).

Treatment with grease patties can be continuous. (If Terramycin is added to control American foulbrood, patties should be taken off during times of surplus honey production.)

(2) Menthol Treatments. A 1.8 oz (50 grams) packet of menthol crystals in a porous bag (such as a paper towel) per two-story colony is put on in the spring or secondarily in the fall. Leave the packet on for 14–28 days with the entrance reduced. Above 80°F, put the packet on the bottom board. Below 80°F, place the packet on the top of the brood nest. Menthol vaporization can be erratic and may require fine-tuning in different areas.

INSECT PESTS OF HONEY BEES

The Small Hive Beetle

Description and Symptoms. The Small Hive Beetle (SHB) (*Aethina tumida* Murray) was first identified in the USA in June 1998, and was not initially considered to be a potential pest for United States beekeepers. However, reports showed that significant numbers of hives had died from the predation effects of the larval stages of the small hive beetle, especially in Florida. In South Africa, the SHB is considered a secondary pest attacking small or weak hives. The beetle is in a large group of beetles commonly called Sap Beetles (Nitidulidae), They are not a flashy insect. As are many Sap Beetles, the Small Hive Beetle is a scavenger and can live on other foodstuffs such as decaying melons. Note that

Figure 125. Larval and adult stages of the Small Hive Beetle.

many other types of beetles are found within the hive that do not have harmful effects. If the Small Hive Beetle is suspected, capture some of the adults and send to either a state land grant college or to a state regulatory department for positive identification.

The SHB is commonly found in sub-Saharan Africa with most information coming from South Africa. Adult beetles are black, move rapidly, and are about 1/2" (5 mm) in length. The adults are tough insects. They squirm vigorously when pinched between the fingers and have been reported to climb from alcohol-filled bottles. Development from egg to adult takes from 38–81 days. The larval stage causes the most problems. Larvae seek out honey and pollen on which to feed. Due to feeding activities, honey drips from ruptured cells and ferments. Combs become slimy and messy, frequently causing residing bees to abscond, which leaves the colony's resources even more vulnerable. After completing the feeding stage, beetle larvae leave the colony and pupate in the soil near the colony.

The biggest concern appears to be the feeding effects of the larvae on honeycombs awaiting processing. Beekeepers in hive beetle areas may be forced to reconsider the process of accumulating supers in anticipation of a single extraction process. It may be that frames must be extracted as soon as they are removed from the colony.

Treatment. Currently a formulation of coumaphos is sold under the trade name of Check Mite+®. It is available from common commercial bee supply sources. Be sure that your state has an emergency exemption for using this material.

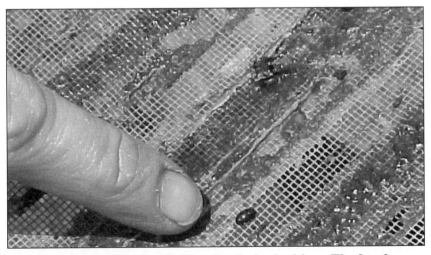

Figure 126. An adult Small Hive Beetle in the hive. The beetles are not large.

For treatment outside the hive, a formulation of permethrin is sold under the trade name of GardStar® 40% EC, which is commonly used to control fire ants and is a soil treatment.

Both of these products are toxic to humans and label instructions should be followed. It should also be noted that USA beekeepers manage a different race of honey bees than in South Africa. The effects of this potential pest are not yet fully known.

Ants

Ants (*Formicidae*) are common intruders within the beehive. Actual damage caused by ants is disputed among beekeepers. Some beekeepers feel that ants are a nuisance to colonies, while other beekeepers feel that ants are of little consequence to beehives. Carpenter ants can cause structural damage to hive equipment, while the common fire ant (*Solenopsis* sp.) can cause painful stings to the beekeeper. Fire ant incubation mounds are frequently found in the bee yard and around beehives. Ironically, there may be some hygienic behavior surrounding this ant and its foraging habits around the hive. Ants remove hive litter in front of the hive and wax moth activity is seemingly minimized in dead equipment. Even so, some beekeepers report that fire ant predation has actually killed colonies.

Treatment. Treatment for ants is difficult. Any pesticide formulation that kills ants in the colony will also kill bees. Setting the hive up on hive stands with legs standing in cans containing motor oil is one way to restrict ants entering the hive. High stands will specifically lessen fire ant activity with beehives, both occupied and empty. Occasionally, beekeepers

Figure 127. Fire ant mounds near the beehive.

will report that Queen Anne's Lace or Wild Carrot (*Daucus carota*) crushed and placed on the inner cover will repel ants.

Wax Moths

The greater wax moth *Galleria mellonella* (L.) is grayish-brown, about 0.75 inch long and has a wingspread of 1.25 inches. The larvae can destroy wax combs in storage or in weak bee colonies by tunneling in the wax. The best control of wax moth larvae in apiaries is to maintain strong colonies. To protect empty wax comb in storage, chemical or non-chemical control can be used. A smaller moth, the Lesser Wax Moth (*Achroia grisella*) can be a problem in stored comb or in live beehives, but the control recommendations are the same.

Figure 128. Combs destroyed by wax moth larvae.

Chemical Control. Currently, the only chemical available for controlling the wax moth is the moth crystal, paradichlorobenzene (PDB). To use PDB, place no more than five deep supers or ten shallow supers in a stack. Seal the cracks between the supers with masking tape or similar material. The stack of supers should be placed on several layers of newspaper or a solid, smooth surface so that the gas cannot escape at the bottom of the stack. Place a piece of paper or cardboard 6 inches square near the center on the top bars in the top super. Put 6 tablespoons (3 ounces) of PDB crystals on this piece of paper. Then put the cover tightly in place. Check each stack every 2 or 3 weeks to be sure that the PDB crystals are still present. If crystals are no longer present, add more. Do not use naphthalene.

PDB is most effective at temperatures above 70°F. A few days before the supers, hive bodies, or combs are to be used, remove them from the stack and set them on end so they can air.

WARNING: PDB can be injurious to man and animals if used improperly. Follow directions and heed all precautions on container label. DO NOT use PDB on honeycombs containing honey intended for human use.

Non-Chemical Control. Temperature extremes can be used as a non-chemical control measure for wax moth control.

Heat. All stages of the greater wax moth are killed at a temperature of 115°F (46°C) for 80 minutes or a temperature of 120°F (49°C) for 40 minutes. Be sure to allow combs to reach the required temperature before measuring the exposure time.

WARNING: Be careful not to expose honeycombs to temperatures in excess of 120°F (49°C). Heat-treat only those combs having little or no honey. Combs, softened at high temperatures, may sag and become distorted. Heat-treat supers of combs only when they are in the normal, upright position. Provide adequate air circulation for the heat to be evenly distributed throughout the comb. Ventilating fans are useful for this purpose. Turn the heat off and allow combs to cool before moving the supers.

Cold. Low temperatures also kill wax moths. The use of low temperatures can prevent the comb sagging problem, which sometimes occurs when combs are treated with heat. Combs with honey and pollen can be treated by use of low temperatures without much danger to the combs. Once the combs are treated, store them where no adult wax moths can get to them. Inspect combs monthly for any signs of infestation, especially if temperatures rise above 60°F. Cold honeycombs are brittle. The minimum temperature and exposure time needed to destroy all stages of the greater wax moth are shown in the following table[15].

Time and Temperature Required
To Kill All Stages of the Wax Moth

Temperature	Time In Hours
20°F (- 7°C)	4.5
10°F (-12°C)	3.0
5°F (-15°C)	2.0

Animal Pests in the Bee Hive

Animals such as raccoons, mice, and skunks are frequent nocturnal pests of hives. Though snakes may occasionally take up temporary residence, mice are the most common internal invaders of the hive. Their small size is the primary reason.

---

[15]*Controlling the Greater Wax Moth.* USDA ARS. Publication 1111. 1984. Out-of-Print.

Mice. Mice will occupy a hive nearly anytime of the year. Cool seasons are by far the most common time for mice to enter the hive. During autumn, mice will search for a place to pass the winter and construct nests in corners of the beehive while the bees are clustered. Though people have the impression that bees will attack and repel such intruders, in fact, mice will be tolerated during cold weather. Mice are obnoxious within the hive. They destroy frames and comb with their nest construction and brood rearing activities. Additionally, mice eat pollen and honey within the wintering hive, thereby keeping the cluster agitated. No doubt, wintering stores are used more quickly due to the increased level of disruption.

Figure 129. A mouse nest in a wintering bee hive.

Keeping mice from entering the hive is relatively simple. Most hive kits are provided with entrance reducers that restrict mice from entering. Too often, beekeepers think that such reducers are for wintering warmth just as a homeowner would close the front door on a cold winter's day. Many types of entrance reducers have been devised.

Nearly all reducers restrict the entrance to one having less than 3/8" openings. Many bottom boards are reversible having a 3/4" side for warm weather and a 3/8" side for cold weather. It is important to install entrance reducers (mouse guards) before the animal occupies the hive. If mouse guards are installed after the mice are in the colony, they are trapped within the colony. The bees will kill the invaders early next spring, but the mice will cause tremendous confusion to the wintering colony before the bees are able to break their wintering cluster.

Skunks and Raccoons. Larger animals such as skunks and raccoons are seasonal pests of the hive as well. These animals cause their problems from the outside of the hive and are predominantly warm weather pests. These animals scratch or otherwise annoy the colony causing bees to come to the colony's defense. Marauding skunks will roll bees on the ground and eat them. In doing so, skunks and raccoons are stung repeatedly, both inside and outside their bodies.

Raising the hive off the ground will help, but may cause the colony to be uncomfortably high when supering. Various types of skunk guards are available and work with varying degrees of success. Beekeepers have reported that putting the colony on a cement slab or putting paver stones in front and sides of the hive eliminate skunk predation. Sometimes beekeepers will either trap or poison pest animals. Be certain that no state regulations are violated when using such extreme control measures.

Other Hive Pests. Birds, toads, coyotes, spiders, lizards, and wasps (yellowjackets) are occasionally observed taking a bee meal. Though annoying, and not beneficial to the colony, such predation is not overly serious. If a unique situation arises where the predation is extreme, contact the county extension office for additional assistance.

Africanized Honey Bees in the US

When the Africanized honey bee (AHB) arrived in the USA, the event was called "the biggest thing ever to happen in entomology." The mid-1950s genesis of the infamous bee was firmly rooted in solid science —to develop a honey bee better suited to tropical conditions than the honey bee that was then in use in Brazil. Things went dramatically awry. Many points in the early history of the Africanization of honey bees have multiple versions of what happened.

Some would say that the story all began much earlier than the 1956–57 period, when the bee first made the Brazilian media. Honey bees are not native to any of America. When a honey bee is seen foraging on a blossom, it will only be the genus and species, *Apis mellifera*, (the common honey bee) which is the only true honey bee in the Americas. Judging from cargo manifests of early merchant ships, honey bee colonies were brought to North America in the 1600s with the colonists. For the most part, they came during the winter, so the bees would be inactive during the cold weather trip. Some historical researchers have reported that the hives were packed in large barrels, as was practically everything else during that time.

These early honey bees were brought from temperate Europe to temperate North America and even today are generally called European bees (EHB). By the 1900s, honey bees had long been established in all three Americas. As understanding of apiculture grew, so did the awareness that the temperate honey bee population established in tropical American areas was probably not the best bee for those areas. African races of honey bees are much more in tune with the differences of climate, pests, and seasons of the tropical climate. Brazilian scientists felt that incorporating some of the attributes of the tropical bee types into the honey bee population in Brazil would result in a better honey bee for the American tropics. Strains of honey bees from Africa were subsequently imported into Brazil for that purpose.

Figure 130. Beekeepers surrounded by Africanized honey bees.

From the 1600s until the present, American beekeepers have selected honey bees to be too big, too yellow, too gentle, and produce too much honey.

The Africanized honey bee would move out of the hive quickly and search for another home if food was unavailable or if pests invaded the hive. Essentially, the African bees in South America were more mobile. The new African bee in Brazil had another characteristic known as vigorous colony defense. Only occasional notice was paid in the North American media to the incidental report of the unusually defensive bees that were causing havoc in Brazil. It was not until the early 1970s that a group of USA scientists made the trip to Brazil to see the defensive, skittish "Brazilian" honey bee. Their conclusions were alarming. The Africanized honey bee in the USA could cause considerable disruption.

Now, in retrospect, the arrival of the Africanized honey bee in this country seems exaggerated, but it was not. These were not good bees to manage for honey production, commercial pollination, or to keep near neighbors. The public will not tolerate excessive stinging attacks. The AHB swarms too much, is too defensive, and absconds (abandons the hive) readily. Essentially, the AHB is an unimproved variety of honey bee. Though the movement may once again start up, the Africanized honey bee has not moved much beyond Houston, Texas but has colonized parts of New Mexico, Arizona, California and Nevada. In recent years, the AHB issue has changed from one of a national concern to a regional concern. Novice beekeepers living in areas that have been Africanized should be much more careful about picking up swarms or taking bees from a building. The biology of this bee is a bit different from that of the more docile European honey bee.

Honey Bee Disease and Pest Identification[16]

Many states have inspection and identification programs to varying degrees. It is to the beekeeper's advantage to work with the respective state organization first before searching for out-of-state sources. However, the USDA Agricultural Research Service has historically offered a disease and pest diagnostic service. Disease samples can be sent to:

Bee Disease Diagnosis
Bee Research Laboratory
Beltsville Agricultural Research Center-East
Building 476
Beltsville, MD 20705

Mail the sample in a heavy box, either cardboard or wood. Loosely wrap the sample in a paper bag, paper towel or newspaper. Avoid plastic bags, aluminum foil, waxed paper or glass because they allow fungi to grow on the samples. Include a description of the problem and return address. The sample should be about 4 inches square and should not contain honey. If adult bees need to be sent, include about 100 dead bees in 70% alcohol. Use heavy leak-proof containers.

---

[16]*Diagnosis of Honey Bee Diseases, USDA Agricultural Research Service, Agricultural Handbook #690.*

CHAPTER 28

Honey Bees and Pesticides

Honey bees and other insect pollinators play an important role in the production of many crops in the USA. However, since most crops are protected from insect pests and diseases, pesticide poisoning is the most serious problem for pollinating insects in agricultural areas. Protecting pollinators, especially honey bees, from pesticide poisoning should be part of any pesticide program. The following recommendations can help minimize bee kills.

Pesticides on Blossoms. The blossom is usually the only part of a plant that bees visit. To avoid killing bees, do not apply pesticides hazardous to bees during the blooming period. When the treated area contains the only attractive plants, in bloom, injury may occur to colonies several miles away. Treating non-blooming crops with a hazardous pesticide when cover crops, weeds, or wild flowers are in bloom within (or near) the treated field may also cause heavy bee losses.

Pesticide Drift. Drift occurs from nearly all spray or dust applications of pesticides from a short distance to miles downwind. Pesticide dusts drift farther than sprays. Pesticides applied by plane usually drift farther than those applied by ground equipment. Generally, it is less hazardous to apply pesticides near apiaries with ground equipment than by plane. Drift can be reduced by applying pesticides in the evening or early morning when the air is calm.

Time of Application.
Ideally, pesticides should be applied when there is no wind and when bees are not visiting plants in the area. The time and intensity of bee visitation to a given crop depends on the abundance and attractiveness of the bloom. For example, apple trees or clover in bloom may be attractive to bees all day while cucumbers and corn are usually attractive in the morning and early afternoon hours. In general, evening or early night applications are the least harmful to bees.

Figure 131. Bees killed by an insecticide.

Formulation of Pesticides. Dusts are usually more hazardous to bees than sprays. Wettable powders often have a longer residual effect than emulsifiable concentrates. Granular pesticides seem to present minimal hazards. Ultra-low volume (ULV) formulations of some pesticides are much more toxic than regular sprays. No effective repellent has been developed that can be added to pesticides to keep bees from treated areas.

Toxicity of Pesticides. Most agricultural pesticides have been tested for their toxicity to honey bees. However, laboratory and field results do not always coincide, due to peculiarities of bee behavior, length of residual life of the pesticide, or the effects of different formulations.

Insecticides affect bees in one or more ways: as stomach poisons, as contact poisons, and as fumigants. Pyrethroids, organophosphates, and carbamates vary in their toxicity to bees from relatively nonhazardous to highly hazardous, depending upon the individual material or combination of materials. Some bacteria, protozoans, and viruses that are currently recommended for biological control pose a serious hazard to bees.

Herbicides, defoliants, and desiccants such as paraquat, MAA, and MSMA are extremely toxic when fed to newly emerged worker honey bees or when sprayed on bees. Other materials in this class are non-hazardous to bees, except that they kill or damage nectar or pollen producing plants.

Fungicides seem to cause little trouble for bees. Captan® at field dosages has caused brood damage.

Sex lures, attractants, and other hormones usually cause no problem for bees. Occasionally, a few honey bees and bumblebees are found in traps containing Japanese beetle lures.

Precautions for Farmers and Applicators:

1. Apply pesticides only when needed.
2. Use the recommended pesticide at the lowest effective rate.
3. Use the pesticide least hazardous to bees that will control the pest involved. If all recommended pesticides are equally hazardous to bees, use the one that has the shortest residual effect.
4. Use sprays or granules instead of dusts.
5. Use ground equipment instead of aerial application to apply pesticides near beehives.
6. Apply pesticides in late afternoon or at night when bees are not working the blooms.
7. Avoid drift of pesticides onto plants that are attractive to bees.
8. Notify beekeepers several days before applying any pesticide that is hazardous to honey bees. This will give them a chance to protect

their colonies. However, notifications are not a release of responsibility.

Precautions for Beekeepers:

1. Place colonies where they will be away from fields that are routinely treated with hazardous pesticides and will not be subjected to pesticide drifts.
2. Identify the apiary. Post the beekeeper's name, address, and phone number in a conspicuous place near the apiary. Let farmers and pesticide applicators know where apiaries are located so they will not poison them.
3. Be familiar with pesticides commonly used in the area and what their application dates are.
4. Relocate colonies that are exposed repeatedly to hazardous pesticides. Also, remember that soon after colonies are moved to a new location, foraging bees search for water. They may collect water that has been contaminated with pesticides. To reduce the chance of bee losses, provide clean water near the hives.

Bee Kill Estimations

0–100 dead bees per day–Normal Die-off
200–400 dead bees per day–Low Kill
500–900 dead bees per day–Moderate Kill
1000 or more dead bees per day–High Kill

If a serious pesticide kill is experienced and the pesticide responsible is unknown, dead bee samples must be sent to chemical laboratories for analysis. This service is for hire and is not always easily obtainable. Contact the county extension office for assistance.

The Insecticide Container Label

Though not a long document, the insecticide label represents vast amounts of research, legal regulations, and instructions. There are thousands of registered pesticide formulations. Each label clearly gives a brand name in bold letters across the label while the common name and chemical ingredients follow in the section called Active Ingredients.

Toxicity of Specific Pesticides

The availability and toxicity of individual pesticides varies greatly. There are hundreds of chemical compounds to be evaluated. Comprehensive lists and toxicity analysis are reviewed and recompiled annually. To obtain a current copy of the list of toxicity levels various pesticides pose to honey bees, contact the county extension office or contact J. Tew.[17]

---

[17]*Write For: Pesticide List, Dr. James E. Tew, Department of Entomology, The Ohio State University, Wooster, OH 44691. Email tew.1@osu.edu.*

CHAPTER 29

Beeswax—Production and Processing

Wax is produced as a highly vaporous liquid by four pairs of glands on the bees' bottom side. The liquid wax flows onto eight "mirrors" or shiny plates where it rapidly hardens into a small, white flake. Strangely, bees often drop these flakes where they can be seen on bottom board. They are not retrieved. These discarded wax scales are an indicator that a nectar flow is underway. The wax-secreting bee uses a long spine on her middle leg to pass the crumbly flake to the front legs where it is chewed, hardened a bit. Using jaws that look like a couple of cement workers' trowels, it is molded in the familiar new comb that beekeepers have seen in past spring seasons.

Figure 132. Cakes of rendered beeswax.

Wax is produced only when storage comb is needed. That is usually during spring and early summer in most parts of the USA. Since it takes about 8 pounds of honey to produce one pound of wax, it is a building material that bees do not produce unless it is needed. When a hive becomes packed with honey and nectar, returning field bees, loaded with nectar, have no place to unload. During these times, even the house bees' internal storage structure (the crop) is filled with nectar. During this period, bees that are of the right age, forced to hold surplus nectar, will involuntarily secrete wax. The beekeeper can not make bees secrete wax, short of feeding heavy sugar syrup.

At this point in the crowded hive, the bees do one of three things:

1. If the hive is not given extra space, they do nothing. So part of the honey crop is lost.

2. In early spring, crowded bees will swarm and again, part of the honey crop is lost.
3. The colony is given extra space, so it builds comb and continues to grow.

Before the major flow starts, be sure to give colonies the space they need.

Processing Beeswax

Melting down beeswax is a pleasant process. Beeswax has a pleasant aroma. However, beeswax is highly flammable and can result in a quick, hot fire. In many commercial beekeeping operations, the wax rendering facility is a separate building from the main facility. Beeswax melts at 147° F and molten wax floats on water. Beekeepers having only a few hives can render a small amount of wax in a double boiler where it can be ladled off and allowed to solidify into molded beeswax cakes. For larger operations, there are many models of melting devices that can be used to melt beeswax. Though most of these devices require hot water to accomplish wax rendering, some wax melters use hot air as the heat source. Wax is extremely durable and stable, but will readily absorb residues from surrounding chemical sources.

Figure 133. A solar wax melter.

A popular melting device for the hobby beekeeper is the solar wax melter. It is primarily a box, painted black on the outside and white on the inside with a glass covering. The box is normally tilted in order for melted wax to run out into a collection pan. Many times, discarded refrigerators with the door replaced with a double glass cover have been modified into solar wax melters. Other beekeepers have put their melters on pivot posts to have the melter always facing the sun.

Though solar wax melters are extremely cheap to use, they are inefficient. Probably only about 50% of the wax is recovered from a solar melter. Additionally, old hard combs are nearly impossible to melt in solar melters.

Slumgum. Slumgum is that ugly residue that clings to the bottom of a rough-rendered cake of beeswax. It is made up of everything that is not honey and wax, though it includes a significant amount of wax. As it builds up inside the melter, it begins to form an insulating layer between the heat and the wax to be rendered. Melters require frequent cleaning. Having a large content of cocoons and hive litter, the dark slumgum can be pressed under pressure in order to yield more wax. Other than being an excellent fire starter for wintertime fires, slumgum has little use.

Beeswax Candles

In years past, the production of beeswax candles was a prominent reason for keeping bees. Even today, beeswax candles are high quality candles that are nearly smokeless and dripless. Candles can be either poured or dipped. Poured candles are generally smoother, but may not have the character that hand-dipped candles have. Though still available new, candle-pouring molds are frequently seen in antique shops and are expensive. Candle making is an aspect of beekeeping that many people do without ever owning a hive.

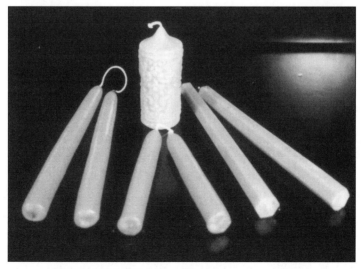

Figure 134. High quality beeswax candles.

The Candle Wick. Clearly, a wick is required for a candle to burn. The wick absorbs the wax in a liquid form and burns the molten beeswax absorbed by the wick. Too large a wick and the candle sides burn out from excessive heat, while too small a wick results in a hole burning down the center of the candle until the flame is extinguished. All wicking today is braided. When burned, braided wicking curls to one side and does not require frequent trimming (snuffing). Wicking can be purchased from candle supply stores or from craft shops. Specify the diameter of the candle to be made when purchasing wicking.

Hand-Dipped Beeswax Candles. Always remember that beeswax is highly flammable. When making simple hand-dipped candles, liquefy enough beeswax to yield the length of candle desired in a non-ferrous container. Attach a weight to the end of the wicking and dip the weighted wick into the molten wax to the depth desired. Pull the wick from the molten wax and wait a few seconds for the hot wax to solidify. Then dip and wait, dip and wait until the desired size candle is produced. This procedure does not guarantee a perfect candle, but a functional candle will be dipped.

Poured Candles. Depending on the mold, either tin or rubber, thread the wicking through the mold and pour the molten wax into the mold. Craft stores sell a candle release compound so the wax will not stick to the mold. After thoroughly cooling, open the mold (if possible) and remove the candles. In many cases, poured candles will be attached by the wicking and will require cutting the wick in order to get two candles.

Beeswax Foundation Candles. Beeswax foundation, as is used in frames, can be rolled around a wick to produce a beeswax candle. This candle will burn more quickly than either a hand-dipped or poured candle but does not require any heat or molten wax. Candle sheets come in a variety of colors and foundation candles are easy to make.

Historically, candles have been so important that innumerable molds, forms, dipping vats, and racks exist for speeding the process along. If one develops an interest in candle making, assistance from such devices will become critical. The procedure is the same, only the equipment and output increase.

CHAPTER 30

Propolis—The Hive's Caulking Compound

Propolis is little known outside of the inner circles of beekeeping. A resinous material collected from the buds of trees or from resins of soft-woods, propolis is used to caulk the hive tight. Poplar and pine trees are common sources of propolis for bees. Though stringy and sticky when fresh, propolis dries hard and brittle. It is soluble in alcohol and has a pleasant weedy odor. Since there is no difference between the two, both wild and managed bees will collect propolis. Caucasian bees are renowned for collecting copious amounts of propolis and can nearly close an entire colony entrance if left to their own schemes. Propolis is the material that causes the hive to crack sharply when opened. Propolis is the primary demon that relegated so many hive designs to beekeeping's junk heap. If colonies are not opened for several years, propolis will make the hive nearly indestructible. Propolis, along with pollen, darkens white wax over a period of just a few years. In addition to being used to polish cells, propolis is added to the wax that covers cappings, therefore giving them a different appearance than honey cappings.

Figure 135. Propolis deposits along the edge of the hive body and on frame edges.

Though the common ingredients of propolis may vary from source to source, generally the major components are plant resins, terpenes, volatile oils, and a few miscellaneous trace materials. Beeswax is major component of propolis within the colony, but is strictly added by the bees. Since propolis is essentially a mix of natural polymers, making it highly insoluble and inert, it is only used for structural purposes within the hive and has no food value.

Propolis is bacterially active and will restrict bacterial growth. Historically, propolis has a long legacy of being useful within early medical procedures for sore throats, skin ailments, burns, gum diseases, and wound dressings. Occasionally, toothpaste products are available that have propolis as part of the ingredients, but these products are rare in the USA. Propolis is not toxic to humans when taken in small amounts.

Propolis has other non-medical uses. A common use is to make a simple varnish, but it can take several weeks for the propolis-based varnish to dry properly.

Probably due to its antibiotic characteristic, propolis is used to entomb anything the bees cannot move—such as a dead mouse or a small tree twig. Varnishing the internal hive surfaces with propolis no doubt provides some antibacterial protection from other pathogens.

Propolis Collection. Propolis scrapings can be saved and heated to melt them into a clump. The contamination of propolis with other detritus such as wood chips, insect parts, or excessive wax will lower its rendered value. To intentionally collect propolis from the bees, a clean 3/4" pine board, having several saw cuts (kerfs), is laid on the top bars of the hive. Since bees dislike cracks in the hive, they will fill the saw cuts with propolis during times of the year when propolis is being gathered. A plastic grid is also available from bee supply sources that bees will fill in the same manner. After the collection device is filled, freeze it. While still frozen, sharply rap the board on a table or twist the plastic propolis collector. Clean propolis chips will break out.

Figure 136. Two propolis traps—a wooden block and a plastic grid.

CHAPTER 31

Starting and Maintaining a Small Observation Hive

Observation hives interest most people. They give one a chance to see bees up close and free from the threat of stings. Since it is normally a small hive with few parts, new beekeepers frequently assume that it will be a simple hive to initiate and operate. That is not true. Glass-walled observation hives are an unnatural environment for a bee nest. If one plans to maintain a permanent observation hive, one needs to be skilled in both bee biology and behavior and have a good observation hive design. Observation hives differ from standard colonies in several major ways.

Figure 137. An observation hive in the Auburn University arboretum.

Light. Light allows the observer to see every part of the observation hive and see the bees' activities. The problem for the bee nest within the observation hive is that bees prefer their hives to be dark. In fact, light inhibits the production of wax. Yet, without light, there is no observation hive. Since bees avoid light, observation hive sides should be covered by panels made of hardboard or expanded-foam insulation when the bees' activities are not being viewed.

Size. Observation hives are generally small hives, usually only one deep frame. That makes them lightweight and easy to transport when needed. However, these small hives do not winter well. They are too small to perform cluster mechanics efficiently. Even if the hive is in a warm house, there are potential problems. Bees tend to fly freely on days that are too cold, probably due to the unnatural wintertime heat of the house. Many beekeepers only maintain the colony during warm months. As the winter season approaches, re-combine the observation hive with an established colony. Then next spring, re-establish the observation colony. Of course, a queen will be lost when using this procedure.

An alternative to seasonally breaking down the observation hive is to maintain a hive large enough to support itself through winter months. Such a hive would have to be made of a minimum of three frames and would survive even better if it were as large as nine frames (three frames side by side). Such colonies survive seasonal variations better, but due to their size, they are much more difficult to manage. An increased number of bees reduces the chances of seeing the queen. In such a hive, crowding is common causing spring swarming.

Disease and Pest Control. In any bee colony, diseases and pests must be constantly controlled. However, in the case of a small observation hive, if it was a healthy colony when established, there should be little danger of diseases or mite buildup during the few months it is in operation. With larger observation hives that are maintained throughout the seasons, standard control of mites and other bee diseases is important.

Access. Opening a standard beehive is relatively easy. Just use some smoke and remove the top of the colony. With an observation hive, the hive must be taken either outside or into a darkened room. One must expect a few bees to occasionally get free the room when the hive is opened or moved. Plan accordingly. If bees can be allowed to escape in the building, then the beekeepers can work inside without disassembling the hive. After completing the job, darken the room except for one window. The bees in the room will fly to a window, which can be opened to free the bees. Various types of doors or slots can be developed to allow access for installing mite strips or grease patties on the observation hive body. Such openings are also good for holding a queen cage. However, there are no standard plans for any of these suggestions. Remember that slots and grooves are quickly filled with propolis or burr comb in the observation bee colony.

Feeder Access. Preparations must be made that allow quick and efficient feeding device installation. Bee populations in observations are small requiring that they fed frequently. If observation hives are wide enough, holes (2-7/8" diameter) can be cut in the top to accommodate common jar or feeder lids. Boardman feeder lids that are already perforated for external hive feeder use are frequently useful for feeding observation hives. Use common jars (e.g. mayonnaise jars) for feeder jars. Ironically, honey jars, having small openings, make good feeder jars. If the hive top is too narrow to accommodate such a large jar, many beekeepers use plastic squeeze bottles with a narrow pointed opening. The squeeze bottle is inverted and its spout is put in a small hole (approximately 1/2") on the hive top.

Figure 138. An observation hive on display.

Ventilation. Observation hives require more ventilation than standard hives. Standard hives usually have cracks and crevices for air to enter or exit. The observation hive is, by design, a tight hive. In addition, the glass walls can catch long-wave radiation and cause excessive heat build-up within the hive. Carbon dioxide build-up can also be problem at any time. Another important consideration is the ventilation "draw" that a highly insulated, tightly built house has. A forceful stream of air can be drawn into the hive entrance, then through the observation hive body, and out the hive's ventilation holes into the house. This is especially serious during cold months when the cluster is trying to regulate its nest temperature. For ventilation holes within the hive body, bore large holes (as large as the sides or top will structurally accommodate) and cover them with 8-mesh hardware cloth. Provide a screened opening near the observation hive entrance to allow air being drawn into the house to escape before being drawn into the observation hive.

Population. The observation hive should not be packed with bees. A hive that is too full of worker bees does not show the other characteristics of bee biology. Ideally, the viewer should be able to see bee dances, wax comb, capped honey, all stages of brood (eggs will be difficult to see), drones, pollen, the queen, which is commonly marked with a spot of enamel paint, and finally, worker honey bees. For a small hive, start it in early spring, after pollen becomes available, with a frame that is approximately 50% covered on both sides with (mostly) capped brood. The frames should have capped honey in the corners. Add enough bees to lightly cover the frames with worker bees. Include a new, marked queen. Feed the new colony. If a hive is set up in the spring, the colony will grow quickly. Once it becomes too full, remove the frame, some of the adult worker bees and allow the process to begin again. Replace the frame with one that is nearly empty. This will give the queen a place to lay eggs and will help to inhibit swarming.

Appearance. The hive should always be maintained correctly. In most cases, an observation hive is a teaching tool for the beekeeper to use when educating the public. If the hive has a layer of dead bees covering the bottom of the hive, the uninformed public can get the wrong impression of bees' worth. In this case, no hive is better than an observation hive in bad shape.

Beekeeper Competence. If a beekeeper can keep an observation hive in good shape all through the year, then the chances for keeping a standard hive alive outside are excellent. Observation hives are somewhat difficult to maintain and are excellent teaching tools for all beekeepers.

CHAPTER 32

Mead—the Honey Wine of the World

Wine, made from honey, is called mead and was the popular drink of Viking explorers. References to mead can be found as far back in recorded history as 334 BC. However, the actual development of mead as a drink is lost in antiquity

As popular as mead has been in the past, it has declined in popularity since the 1700s. Possibly, the increased demand for honey as a sweetener or the increasing availability of high quality wines caused the demand for mead to decline. Mead, of varying quality, can be made from any kind of honey.

Figure 139. Bottles of commercially brewed mead (honey wine).

The Mead Making Process[18]

Honey and water are combined to begin the process of wine making. Usually a dark honey or one with a strong flavor will decrease chances of producing a superior dry wine. Likewise, water contaminated with heavy minerals or other additions may detract from the delicateness or bouquet of the final product. Therefore, a mild-flavored honey and pure chlorine-free water should be used.

When making wine, the sugar source is sterilized. In the case of mead, honey is mead's sugar source and should be heated to kill wild

---

[18] Caron, Dewey M. 1999. Honey Bee Biology and Beekeeping. Wicwas Press, LLC. Cheshire, CT 06510-0817. pp 268-272

yeasts. Sterilization can be accomplished by boiling the sugar and water mixture for a couple of minutes. However, since honey can be adversely affected by such a procedure, boiling is not recommended to produce a decent honey wine. Instead, campden tablets or sodium bisulfite (from wine supply sources) are added to the dilute honey solution. The liberated sulfur dioxide will sterilize the must (honey-water mixture) and kill foreign low-alcohol-tolerant yeasts.

Wine Yeasts. The type of yeast used is probably the most critical factor in regard to mead taste. Baking yeasts and non-cultured yeasts are usually not satisfactory. Suitable pure yeast cultures can be obtained from wine supply firms. An all-purpose wine yeast, Madeira, Tokay, or sherry yeast will give good results. Experimentation will yield the right type for one's taste. The yeast package will recommend the correct amount to use.

Yeast added to any honey water mixture will ferment over time. To hasten fermentation and increase the chances of a successful product, yeast food (urea and ammonium phosphate) and tannin (tea) should be added. Since most wines are acidic, the addition of an acid in the form of tartaric or citric acid is recommended. The ideal mixture should be acidic with a pH of 3.5 or 3% tartaric acid. Most wine makers like to start their yeast cultures in a small portion (5–10%) of the final mixture for 2–3 days before adding it to the entire mixture. This helps insure a rapid fermentation.

Fermentation. After adding all materials, the mixture should be placed in a non-metallic container that can be fitted with a fermentation lock. The container should be no more than two-thirds full to prevent the must from bubbling over. One- or five-gallon carboys make good containers. If large volumes are made at one time, the initial mix can be put in a crock or polyurethane pail for the first 3–4 days of rapid fermentation before placement in jugs fitted with fermentation locks. This container may be 7/8 full. The fermentation valve permits escape of carbon dioxide without entry of oxygen. A homemade lock consisting of rubber tubing attached to a section of glass tubing in the cork stopper leading down to a small glass jar with enough water to cover the tube ending works satisfactorily. Water should not enter the fermenting mixture.

Fermentation works best at 65° F. A constant temperature is better than a widely fluctuating temperature but temperatures lower than 60° F will lengthen fermentation time. Higher temperatures, up to 85° F, produce a more rapid fermentation. This does not present a problem provided enough yeast nutrients are present in the mixture. The must should have the dead yeast cells and sediment siphoned off after one month. When siphoning, be careful not to disturb the bottom or transfer the material floating at the top. Replace the fermentation lock once again.

Following the end of fermentation, once again pour the clear wine off (called racking the wine). A cloudy wine will clarify with time but a fining agent such as gelatin or commercial clay, from a wine supply company, will accomplish the same purpose. Sterilizing the must mixture before beginning the fermentation aids in securing a clear, non-cloudy final product. The wine should be racked into sterilized bottles or oaken wine casks and corked.

Aging and Serving. Honey wine, like all wines, needs to be aged. Aging bottles should be stored in a cool dry place and left undisturbed in a horizontal position. Bottled sweet cloudy wines might explode due to yeast reactivation. One year is usually sufficient aging time but this is a matter of taste. New wines are yeasty tasting, lack bouquet and are frequently cloudy.

Serving the finished product in wine bottles with distinctive labels is a nice touch. Wine supply firms have bottles, corks and corking devices available. Wines aged in the service bottle will frequently have bottom sediment.

Recipe for Sweet Mead:

1. 3–4 pounds of mild favored honey
2. 1 gallon of water
3. 1/4 ounce citric acid (1 level teaspoon)
4. 1/4 pint strong tea
5. Yeast culture
6. Yeast nutrient salts
7. 1 campden tablet

CHAPTER 33

A Synopsis of Beekeeping's History

The human association with bees is an old one, thus far too complex for a detailed discussion here. Even so, beekeeping's history should not be ignored. For many thousands of years, people hunted bee nests and looted them. Since they practiced no hive management, early beekeepers were appropriately called honey hunters. There is good evidence that humans have had a relationship with honey bee keepers since about 5000BC[19].

Though humans have robbed and manipulated hives for thousands of years, it cannot be said they were fast learners. The most basic aspects of honey bee sociality has only been understood during the past one hundred years. Presently, apicultural scientists are still making advances in areas of behavioral and chemical communication and physiology. The fact that it has taken so long and that the bees are still so undomesticated is a credit to honey bees' stamina for resisting technological advances. However, bee breeders have succeeded in making honey bees larger, sting less, and increased their honey-gathering propensity. Otherwise, they are still the bees that were kept by apicultural ancestors. Bees still sting. Bees still swarm. Bees still forage on plants that they choose. Bees are still undomesticated. At best, they tolerate humans and artificial hive domiciles.

Who deserves to be noted in an overview of beekeeping history? So many people have made so many contributions—both large and small that selecting deserving beekeepers causes problems. However, several names[20] will live for many years in international beekeeping history. These people deserve note.

L. L. Langstroth. If beekeeping history is accepted literally, it took just a little less than 7000 years to figure out the design of a hive, that incorporated bee space, which both beekeepers and bees tolerate. To this day, it is not perfect for either bees or beekeepers. In 1851, L. L. Langstroth recorded his thoughts on the standard hive design and patented his hive ideas. It was probably the greatest contribution ever made to beekeeping, but Langstroth never profited from it. Indeed, he had to spend a great deal of energy defending his patent. Once seen, Langstroth's concepts were obvious to everyone. For his contributions to

---

[19]Graham, Joe (Editor). 1992. *The Hive and the Honey Bee.* Dadant and Sons, Inc. Hamilton, IL. pp 1-13.
[20]Pellet, Frank C. 1946. *A Living From Bees.* Orange Judd Publishing Company, Inc. NY. pp 302-316

beekeeping, L.L. Langstroth is called the "The Father of Modern Beekeeping."

A. I. Root was another beekeeping visionary. At his jewelry factory in Medina, Ohio, a swarm landed near an open window. As with many beekeepers, he had no notion of getting into the beekeeping business until that fateful day. Root is given much of the credit for simplifying Langstroth's hive and manufacturing it commercially. He wrote a bee-keeping periodical (*Gleanings In*) *Bee Culture* and a book, *The ABC & XYZ of Beekeeping*, both of which are still printed today. Presently, Root descendants continue to operate the A. I. Root Company, but not so much in beekeeping as in candle production.

C. P. Dadant was a prominent writer and dedicated student of bee behavior. Though he never spoke the English language competently, he was instrumental in reviewing international bee literature and establishing new beekeeping ideas both in the United States and in Europe. Today, his company, Dadant & Sons, Inc., is one of the largest bee equipment manufacturers in the world.

Samuel Wagner has become less known as the years have passed and will probably continue to approach obscurity, but credit should be given to him for starting publication of the first bee magazine in the English language, *The American Bee Journal.* Today many magazines and web pages are devoted to international beekeeping, but Wagner was the insightful beekeeper who first published an English beekeeping periodical.

Figure 140. An antique hive and skep with a woven super.

Additionally, Wagner was one of the original beekeepers who first imported the Italian honey bee into the USA. Though he was normally in the background, Wagner made a significant long-term contribution to the fledging beekeeping industry.

G. M. Doolittle frequently wrote for bee journals in the early years of beekeeping. He spent the better part of his beekeeping life studying the fundamentals of honey bee queen production and published his observations in *Scientific Queen Rearing*, a text that revolutionized honey bee queen production. The procedure for producing commercial numbers of honey bee queens has changed little to this day. Through the years, millions of queens have been grown and sold using his procedures.

CHAPTER 34

Specialized Pieces of Beekeeping Equipment

A Vacuum Device for Managing Bees

Uses for a Bee Vacuum. A bee vacuum can be used for picking up swarms, removing bees from the walls of buildings, removing bees from flight cages or other research projects, removing bees from honey processing rooms, taking bees off people who have presented bee beard demonstrations, and filling bee package cages.

Figure 141. A shop-built bee vacuum device.

Vacuum Source. The vacuum power can be an electric shop-vacuum or a gasoline-powered tripod bee blower, which is available from commercial bee equipment companies. Normally, a bee blower is used to remove bees from honey supers. In reality, nearly any vacuum device can be modified to provide suction for the vacuum device. The advantages to using an electrically-powered vacuum are reduced vacuum cost and simplicity.

The advantages to modifying a bee blower to provide the vacuum force are that the device is gasoline-powered and will work anywhere. Secondly, it offers another use for what is normally a single-use piece of equipment. The obvious disadvantage is the initial cost of the bee blower and its mechanical maintenance. For those not interested in purchasing a blower or building a vacuum trap, commercially-produced vacuum devices are available.

Modifying the Blower to Accept a 2-1/4" Vacuum Line. A tripod bee blower comes with a simple wire screen covering the air intake hole. This is a safety feature that prevents both bees and fingers from getting into the impeller. Remove this screen and replace it with a plywood board six inches square. Attach the board with 1/4" machine bolts. Be sure that they are clear of the impeller blades. In the center of the board, bore a hole measuring 2-1/4" to accept the vacuum line. Modify the opening to accept the size vacuum line to be used. There is no requirement that a 2 -1/4" hose be used but they are readily available. They do not clog as easily as smaller lines and they give more even vacuum pressure.

Vacuum Hoses. Common 2-1/4" shop-vacuum hoses are used. Extra hoses are available at building supply outlets or hardware stores. Adapters and couplers are available for increasing the length of either the vacuum hose or the trap hose. Plastic piping, of the correct diameter, can be used to make a long, rigid extension tube for retrieving high swarms. This is nothing more than a long nozzle.

The Trap Box. Frequently, a beekeeper simply vacuums bees into a common shop vacuum for subsequent removal. A few bees survive, but most are mangled and killed. It would be comparable to spending about half an hour in a tornado. A trap in the line is necessary to prevent vacuumed bees from passing through the vacuum impeller or being swirled around within the vacuum canister.

Within reason, the trap can be any size. A simple trap can be nothing more than a modified deep hive body, but a better design is a trap made from 3/4" stock with the top and bottom being made from 1/2" plywood. A trap having the inside dimensions of: 14-3/4" wide x 11-1/4" long x 10" deep works well. The photos show a common bee shipping-package in the trap. The beekeeper should select a cage that is common enough to be easily replaced as it becomes worn or filled with bees.

Vacuum force draws the bees into the vacuum hose and dumps them into the shipping package where they are constrained by the screened wire walls of the shipping cage. To allow space for air movement, the shipping package does not fill the entire trap box, but is held in place by two wooden cleats. If the cage is too close to the vacuum line exit, bees will be hopelessly drawn against the wire wall of the shipping cage. Being unable to move away from the vacuum exhaust hole, increasing numbers of bees accumulate and can plug the airflow. The shipping package used at The Ohio State University Honey Bee Laboratory requires space of 14-3/4" wide x 5" long x 10" deep in the trap box. The 6-1/4" space not filled by the shipping package is for air movement and to keep the side of the package a few inches from the exhaust vent hole. The inside lip of the trap is lined with adhesive-backed weather-stripping in order to assure a good vacuum seal.

When considering trap dimensions, consider how the trap will operate near the top of a ladder with a swarm still several feet above and bee blower running, at full throttle down below. Big traps are not always better even though they have more capacity.

Vacuum Line Openings. The vacuum trap line opening in the top is positioned so it is directly over the hole in the shipping cage when the top is in position. The vacuum line hole exiting to the blower is positioned 4" from the trap bottom. All openings are 2-1/4".

Vacuum Pressure Shunt. Frequently, too much vacuum pressure can harm bees. A 2-1/4" opening in the trap top is positioned over the empty space within the trap (i.e. on the opposite side from the trap vacuum line in the top). Bees should not be in this part of the trap. Nevertheless, the shunt hole is covered with 8-mesh hardware cloth. A simple wooden flap is closed to increase vacuum pressure or is opened to bypass the trap vacuum thereby decreasing vacuum pressure. Partially opening or closing the shunt hole will adjust the vacuum pressure. The pressure of the vacuumed air will hold the flap in place while the blower is running.

Vacuum Trap Operation. Bees are drawn, by vacuum pressure, into the hose that the beekeeper uses to pick up bees. Normally the far end of the hose has a nozzle on it, but that is not required. Vacuumed bees tumble down the trap hose and enter the vacuum trap through the top hole. The bees fall into the delivery package where they are confined. The vacuumed air continues to flow from the screened package out the exit hole, through the vacuum line to the blower where air is exhausted from the blower. Ironically, in this bee vacuuming process, this air is considered to be "waste" air. Although when removing bees from honey supers, the exhausted air is the critical principle in blowing bees from supers. Using opposites—vacuuming and blowing—achieves the same goal— removing bees from something.

The amount of pressure needed to vacuum bees can only be learned from experience. If the operator touches the comb with the vacuum nozzle and bees are whisked away effortlessly, there is a good chance the pressure is too high. At the correct vacuum pressure, bees should cling to the comb, holding on for just a second, and then lightly be drawn into the vacuum trap tube. The bees striking the wall of the vacuum trap tube should have a velvety feel while sharp thuds indicate too much vacuum pressure.

Again, only experience can tell the operator when the package is full. The trap vacuum line can be removed—with the blower running. A flashlight can be used to determine how full the package is. Bees are unable to fly or even crawl out of the top opening due to the resistance of the vacuum airflow.

If the airflow is stopped and bees are confined to the trap, they will die within minutes. Confining in the trap with no airflow allows excessive heat to build up within 4–5 minutes if the package is nearly full. As a note of interest, when overheating occurs, drones die first.

Bees that are vacuumed into a shipping package and are immediately released can be particularly aggressive, especially if they were taken from a hive rather than a swarm. Significant stinging occurrences have happened when freshly vacuumed bees are immediately released. Feed packaged bees sugar syrup, keep it dark and cool and allow the bees to settle for a few hours. Then release them.

Removing the Shipping Package from the Trap. Remove the trap vacuum line while the blower is running. Soundly thump the trap on the ground and briskly remove the trap top. Immediately place an appropriately-sized plywood cover onto the package entrance. Remove the shipping package from the trap. The trapped bees can then be released into other beehive equipment.

Slatted Rack

Dr. C.C. Miller[21] first described the slatted rack as a deep bottom board that was two inches deep rather than the standard 3/4" bottom board used today. It is essentially a plain box open at one end. Originally the deep bottom board was to be reversed during warm

Figure 142. A slatted rack resting on a bottom board.

[21]Miller, C.C. (1915) *Fifty Years Among the Bees*, The A. I. Root Company, Medina, OH pp 51-52.

months to a shallow side of 3/4", but Dr. Miller devised a rack to go in the deep side in order to leave the deep bottom in place year round. The rack was made of simple slats (about 21 slats 3/4" wide x 3/8" thick) nailed to two runners that were on either end of the slats. The slats are separated from each other by about 3/8".

Although the deep bottom board rack was never manufactured commercially, several manufacturers still offer a modified version of the slatted rack. Rather than being a deep bottom board, the slats are built in a frame that lies on top of a regular bottom board and is called a board-slatted rack. It is a simple frame grooved on the two long sides. The slats and the entrance board are trapped in those grooves. The entrance board's function is to deflect winter winds and to move bees away from the entrance during warmer weather. The width of the entrance board can vary, but generally, it is about 3/8" x 3" x slat length.

Figure 143. The slatted rack concept.

The deep bottom board was reported to improve wintering, reduce swarming, and prevent overheating. Though not often employed now, the slatted rack appears to be a useful piece of specialized beekeeping equipment.

Drip Board

A drip board is a simple piece of equipment that is nearly always homemade. These rimmed boards are used to stack honey supers on before and after extracting. Honey generally oozes from broken cappings while awaiting uncapping and make a mess on the honey house floor. An upper rim on the board catches and holds honey and wax pieces while two cleats (3/4" x 2") keep the board slightly off the floor. A hand truck nose can be quickly and easily placed under the super stack for moving. Cut either 5/8" or 3/4" plywood to the outside dimensions of a brood chamber (16-1/4" x 19-7/8"). Add a perimeter rim around all edges. The rim should be about 3/4" by 1-1/2". Glue or screw the rim and the bottom cleats to the board. When holding a full stack of supers, the load can be great. In a pinch, drip boards can be used, in the inverted position, as a temporary cover on super stacks in the honey house. These are simple but extremely useful pieces of equipment.

Figure 144. A drip board.

Epilogue

Beekeeping is a pathway. It has a beginning but no ending. To the beginning beekeeper, everything is new, even foreign. Like one learning another language, new beekeepers grow in confidence and skills until they are no longer new beekeepers, but they never stop learning—even as they become old beekeepers.

If a Master Beekeeper from a hundred years ago could return to us, that knowledgeable beekeeper would never have seen Varroa or tracheal mites, insecticides, plastic frames, antibiotics, stainless steel processing equipment, latex paint, or plastic honey jars. Yes, the hypothetical Master Beekeeper would need a beekeeping course.

Beekeeping has changed in many ways during the past hundred years —some subtle while other changes have been abrupt. Yes, there are still mites and other new pests and no, the old pests have not been conquered, though progress has been made.

I no longer attempt to predict beekeeping's future, but I am certain that we have one; however, there was a time just a few years ago, when I was not so certain. Agriculture and society may change, but the bees have been remarkably constant. Although we now understand a lot about the bees' mysteries, we have not yet found the hive's Rosetta stone. We know more but we still do not fully understand.

What if I could visit a future bee operation one hundred years from now? What will beekeeping look like? I have no idea, but I suspect that bees will still forage for pollen and nectar. There will still be flowers and there will still be beekeepers with new problems. If I could visit the future, I know I would be antiquated and the problems of my day would be quaint, but I would be able to talk to those future beekeepers about their bees and I would understand their passion for bees and their ways. I hope that this book has helped to fire your passion for beekeeping.

James E. Tew
The Ohio State University

Appendix 1

POLLEN AND NECTAR SOURCES

Some Major and Minor Sources of Nectar and Pollen Plants

N = Nectar Source

P = Pollen Source

HD = Honeydew Source

MAJOR = Major source of either pollen or nectar

Plant	Nectar/Pollen	Bloom Dates
Alder *Alnus incana*	P	Summer
Alfalfa *Medicago sativa* (Good honey plant)	N & P	Summer
Almond *Prunus amygdalus* Batsch (Major)	N & P	Winter-Spring
Alsike Clover *Trifolium hybridum* (Excellent honey plant) (Major)	N & P	Spring-Summer
Alyssum *Lobularia maritime*	P	Summer-Autumn
American Mountain Ash *Sorbus americana*	P	Spring-Summer
Anise hyssop *Agstache foeniculum*	N	Summer-Frost
Apple (*Malus* spp.) (Major)	N & P	Spring
Arrowleaf Clover *Trifolium vesiculosum* Savi (Yuchi not particularly productive)	N & P	Summer

Asparagus *Asparagus officinalis*	P	Spring-Summer
Aster alpinus *Aster alpinus*	N & P	Summer
Aster *Aster* spp. (Extremely large group. Not all are good nectar sources) (Major)	N & P	Sep-Frost
Autumn Joy *Sedum spectabile*	N & P	Summer-Autumn
Azalea *Rhododendron spp.* (Over 900 species. Some types produce poisonous nectar)	N	Summer
Basswood *Tilia americana* (Good honey plant. Short bloom) (Major)	N & P	Summer
Beggar's-tick *Bidens alba* L.	N	Summer
Birdsfoot trefoil *Lotus corniculatus* L.	N	Summer
Bitterweed *Helenium amarum*	N & P	Spring-Summer
Black Locust *Robinia pseudoacacia* (Mainly nectar. Short bloom period)	N & P	Spring-Summer
Black Chokeberry *Aronia melanocarpa*	N	Spring-Summer
Blackberry *Rubus* spp. (Major)	N & P	Spring-Summer
Black Haw *Viburnum prunifolium*	N	Spring-Summer

Black Mangrove *Avicennia germinans* L. (Major)	N	Summer
Blue Curls *Trichostema lanceolatum* Benth.	N & P	Summer
Blue Vervain *Verbena hastata* L.	N	Summer
Blueweed *Echium vulgare* (Also Viper's Bugloss)	N	Summer
Blueberry *Vaccinium corymbosum*	N	Spring-Summer
Boneset *Eupatorium* spp. (Also White Snakeroot, Joe-Pye weed)	N & P	Summer-Autumn
Borage *Borago officinalis*	N & P	Summer-Frost
Boston Ivy *Parthenocissus tricuspidata*	N & P	Summer
Box Elder *Acer negundo* L.	N & P	Spring
Brazilian Pepper *Schinus terebinthifolius* Raddi (Also Florida Holly. Peppery-tasting honey)	N	Summer-Autumn
Brazilian Pusley *Richardia brasiliensis* (Moq.)	N	Summer-Autumn
Bronze Bugle *Ajuga reptans*	N & P	Spring
Buckwheat *Fagopyrum esculentum* (Unique and strongly flavored honey)	N & P	Summer
Buckwheat Tree *Cliftonia monophylla* (Lam.) Britt	N	Winter-Spring

Buckthorn *Rhamnus spp.*	N	Summer-Autumn
Bur Clover *Medicago hispida* Gaertn.	N	Spring-Summer
Burdock *Arctium minus* (Hill) Bernh.	N & P	Summer
Burford Chinese Holly *Ilex cornuta 'Burfordii'*	N & P	Spring
Burnet *Sanguisorba* spp.	P	Summer
Buttonbush *Celphalanthus occidentalis* L.	N	Spring-Summer
Buttercup *Ranunculus* spp.	N & P	Spring
Butterfly Weed *Asclepias tuberosa*	N	Summer
Cabbage *Brassica oleracea* L.	N & P	Spring-Summer
Cabbage Palm *Sabal palmetto* (Walt) (Major)	N	Summer
Cactus, Prickly-pear *Opuntia* spp.	N & P	Spring-Summer
California Buckeye *Aesculus californiaca* (Spach) Nutt. (Toxic to Bees)	N & P	Summer
California Laurel *Umbellularia californica*	N & P	Winter-Spring
California Poppy *Eschscholtzia californica*	P	Spring-Summer
Candytuft *Iberis sempervirens*	N	Spring

Canola *Brassica napus* L. (Honey granulates quickly)	N & P	Spring-Summer
Caragana *Caragana arborescens* L & M (Also Siberian pea)	N & P	Summer
Carolina Laurelcherry *Prunus caroliniana*	N & P	Spring
Carrot *Daucus carota* L.	N & P	Summer
Cascara *Rhamnus purshiana* DC	N & P	Spring-Summer
Cattail *Typha latifolia*	P	Summer
Catalpa *Catalpa speciosa* (Also Indian Bean)	N & P	Summer
Catmint *Nepeta grandiflora* (Also Catnip)	N	Summer
Ceanothus *Ceanothus* spp.	N & P	Spring
Cedar, Incense *Calocedrus decurrens* (Torr.) Florin	HD	Winter-Spring
Celery *Apium graveolens* L.	N	Summer
Chaparral Broom *Baccharis pulularis* DC	N & P	Summer
Chaste Tree *Vitex agnus-castus*	N & P	Spring-Summer
Cherry (Cultivated) *Prunus cerasus*	N & P	Spring
Chestnut *Castanea dentata*	P	Spring-Summer

Chickweed *Stellaria media*	N & P	Spring-Frost
Chickory *Cichorium intybus* L.	N & P	Summer-Frost
Chinese Tallow Tree *Sapium sebiferum*	N	Spring-Summer
Chinquapin *Castanopsis chrysophylla* Dougl.	N & P	Spring-Summer
Chives *Allium schoenoprasum*	N & P	Spring-Summer- Autumn
Citrus *Citrus* spp. (Orange, Lemon, Lime, Grapefruit)	N & P	Spring-Summer
Clematis *Clematis ligusticifolia* Nutt.	N & P	Summer
Cleome, Yellow *Cleome lutea* Hook.	N & P	Spring-Frost
Clethra Summersweet *Clethra alnifolia*	N	Summer
Clover *Trifolium* spp. (large group, generally productive)	N & P	Spring-Summer
Coffee Berry *Rhamnus californica* Esch.	N & P	Spring-Summer
Common Hackberry *Celtis occidentalis*	N & P	Spring
Common Vetch *Vicia cracca* L.	N & P	Summer
Coral Vine *Antigonon leptopus* Hook. & Arn.	N	Nearly all year

Corneliancherry Dogwood *Cornus mas*	N & P	Spring
Corny Mock Orange *Philadelphus coronarius* L.	N	Summer
Cotoneaster *Cotoneaster* spp.	N & P	Spring-Summer
Cotton *Gossypium hirsutum*	N & P	Summer-Autumn
Cottonwood *Populus* spp.	P	Spring
Crab Apple *Malus* spp.	N & P	Spring-Summer
Crocus *Crocus vernus*	P	Spring
Cucumber *Cucumis sativus* (Require pollination, but rarely provide surplus honey)	N & P	Summer
Dandelion *Taraxicum officinale* (secondary bloom through frost) (Major)	N & P	Spring
Dead Nettle *Lamium purpureum* L.	N & P	Spring
Devils-walkingstick *Aralia spinosa* (Also Hercules-club)	N	Summer
Dodder *Cuscuta* spp.	N	Summer-Autumn
Dogbane *Apocynum* spp.	N & P	Summer
Douglas Fir *Pseudotsuga menziesii*	P	Spring

Downingia *Downingia elegans* (Lindl.)Torr.	N	Summer
Elderberry *Sambucus* spp. (American Elder, Blue Elder)	P	Summer
Elm *Ulmus americana*	P & HD	Winter-Spring
English Ivy *Hedera helis* L.	N & P	Autumn-Winter
Eriogonum, White *Eriognum niveum* Dougl.	N & P	Summer
Eucalyptus *Eucalyptus* spp.	N & P	Winter-Spring- Summer
Evening Primrose *Oenothera* spp.	P	Spring-Summer
Everlasting, Pearly *Anaphalis margaritacea*(L.)B.&H.	N & P	Summer
Fairwell-to-Spring *Clarkia amoena* (Lehm.)Nels.	P	Summer
False Indigo *Amorpha fruticosa* L.	N & P	Spring
Fedderbush *Lyonia lucida* (Lam.) (Bitter Honey)	N	Spring
Figwort *Scrophularia* spp.	N	Spring-Summer
Filaree *Erodium cicutarium*(L.) L'Her.	N & P	Spring
Fireweed *Epilobium angustifolium* L. (Major)	N & P	Summer
Flat-topped Goldenrod *Euthamia minor* (Michx.)	N	Summer-Autumn

Flax *Linum usitatissimum* L.	N & P	Summer
Florida Pusley *Richardia scabra* (Also Florida Purslan)	N	Spring-Summer- Autumn
Gallberry *Ilex glabra* (Also Inkberry) (Major)	N & P	Spring
Garlic Chives *Allium tuberosa*	N & P	Summer-Autumn
Germander *Teucrium chamaedrys*	N & P	Summer
Gill-Over-The-Ground *Nepeta glechoma* (Also Ground Ivy)	N & P	Spring-Summer
Globe Thistle *Echniops ritro*	N	Summer
Golden Currant *Ribes aureum* Pursh.	N	Summer
Goldenrod *Solidago* spp. (Good fall nectar plant. Honey has strong odor) (Major)	N & P	Autumn
Gopher Apple *Licania michauxii* Prance	N	Spring
Hairy Vetch *Vicia villosa*	N & P	Summer
Hawthorn *Crataegus* spp.	N & P	Spring
Hazelnut *Corylus* spp. (Also Filbert. Marginal pollen producer)	P	Winter-Spring
Heartsease *Polygonum* spp. (Also Smartweed. Mainly honey plant)	N & P	Spring-Summer- Autumn

Hickory *Hicoria* spp. (Erratic producer. Low quality honey)	HD	Summer-Autumn
Holly *Ilex opaca* (Also American Holly)	N & P	Spring-Summer
Honey Locust *Gleditsia triancanthos* (Also Thorny Locust. Rarely surplus)	N & P	Spring-Summer
Hop Clover *Trifolium procumbens* (marginal nectar & pollen plant)	N & P	Summer
Hop-Tree *Ptelea trifoliata*	N	Summer
Horehound *Marrubium vulgare*	N	Summer
Horse Chestnut *Aseculus hippocastanum* L.	N & P	Spring
Horsemint *Monarda* spp.	N & P	Spring-Summer- Autumn
Hungarian Speedwell *Veronica latifolium*	N	Summer
Ironweed *Vernonia* spp.	N & P	Spring-Summer- Autumn
Jewelweed *Impatiens pallida* Nutt.	N & P	Summer-Autumn
Knapweed *Centaurea* spp.	N	Summer
Korean evodia *Evodia daniellii*	N	Summer-Autumn
Kudzu *Pueraria thunbergiana* A. & Z. Benth.	N & P	Spring
Lambs Ears *Stachys byzantina*	N	Spring-Summer

Land-In-Blue *Aster x dumosus*	N & P	Summer-Autumn
Lavender *Lavendula augustifolia*	N	Summer-Autumn
Leadwort *Amorpha fruticosa* (Also Indigobush Amorpha, Bastard Indigo)	N & P	Summer
Leopards Bane *Doronicum cordatum*	N & P	Spring
Lespedeza *Lespedeza* spp.	N & P	Spring-Summer- Autumn
Lima Bean *Phaseolus lunatus* L.	N & P	Spring-Summer
Loganberries *Rubus ursinus*	N & P	Spring-Summer
Lungwort *Pulmonaria* spp.	N	Spring
Mallow *Malva alcea* "Fastigiata"	P	Summer-Autumn
Majoram *Origanum vulgare* L.	N	Summer
Manzanita *Arctostaphylos* spp.	N & P	Spring
Maple *Acer* spp. (Rarely honey) (Major)	N & P	Winter-Spring
Mauve Catmint *Nepeta mussinii* (Also Persian Catmint, Catnip)	N	Summer-Autumn
Mesquite *Prosopis* spp.	N & P	Spring-Summer
Mexican Clover *Richardia scarbra* L.	N	Spring-Autumn

Milk Vetch *Astragalus* spp. (Also Loco Weed, Rattle Weed)	N	Spring-Summer
Milkweed *Asclepias* spp. (mainly nectar plant)	N & P	Summer
Mistletoe *Phoradendron flavescens*	P	Spring
Mountain Bluet *Centaurea montana*	N	Spring
Mountain Mint *Pycnanthemum flexuosum*	N	Summer-Frost
Mountain Laurel *Kalmia latifolia* L. (Reported to produce poisonous honey)	N	Spring-Summer
Mullein *Verbascum thapsus* L.	N & P	Summer
Muskmelon *Cucumis* spp. (Includes Honey Dew, Cantaloupes)	N & P	Summer-Frost
Mustard *Brassica* spp.	N & P	Spring
Nuttall's Thistle *Cirsium nuttallii* DC	N	Spring
Oak *Quercus* spp. (Low quality honey crop)	HD& P	Spring-Summer- Autumn
Ohio Buckeye *Aesculus glabra* (Also Horse Chestnut)	N & P	Spring-Summer
Onion *Alium* spp.	N & P	Spring
Oregano *Origanum vulgare*	N	Summer-Autumn

Palmetto *Salbal* spp.	N & P	Spring-Summer
Parsley *Petroselinum crispum*	N & P	Summer
Parsnip *Pastinaca sativa* L.	N &P	Spring
Partridge Pea *Chamaecrista fasciculata* (Michx.)	N	Summer-Autumn
Peach *Prunus persica*	N & P	Spring
Pear *Pyrus communis* (Poor nectar producer)	N & P	Spring
Peppermint *Mentha peperita* L.	N & P	Summer
Peppervine *Ampelopsis arborea* (L.)	N	Spring-Summer
Phacelia *Phacelia* spp.	N & P	Spring-Summer
Persimmon *Diospyros virginiana*	N	Spring-Summer
Philippine Chaste Tree *Vitex negundo* L.	N	Summer-Autumn
Pine *Pinus* spp. (Honeydew crop rarely)	P & HD	Summer
Plantain *Plantago* spp.	P	Spring-Summer
Plum *Prunus* spp.	N & P	Spring
Poison Oak *Rhus diversiloba*	N & P	Spring-Summer
Pot Marigold *Calendula officinalis*	N & P	Summer

Privet *Ligustrum* spp.	N & P	Summer
Pumpkin *Cucurbita pepto* (Also Squash and Gourds)	N & P	Summer-Frost
Punk Tree *Melaleuca quinquenervia* (Also Cajeput, Melaleuca) (Major)	N	Summer
Purple Loosestrife *Lythrum salicaria* L. (This is a noxious exotic plant and should not be planted.)	N	Summer
Pussy Willow *Salix discolor*	N & P	Winter-Spring
Pyracantha *Pyracantha* spp.	N & P	Spring-Summer
Quince *Cydonia oblonga* Mill.	N & P	Spring
Rabbit Brush *Chrysothamnus* spp.	N & P	Summer
Radish *Raphanus sativus* L.	N & P	Spring-Summer
Ragweed *Ambrosia trifida*	P	Summer
Raspberry *Rubus* spp. (Also Thimbleberry)	N	Spring-Summer
Red Bud *Cercis canadensis* (Also Judas Tree)	N & P	Spring
Red Cedar *Juniperus virginiana* (Honey dew crop rarely)	HD	Summer-Autumn
Red Chokeberry	N	Spring-Summer

Aronia arbutifolia		
Red Clover *Trifolium pratense* L.	N	Summer
Red-Flowering Thyme *Thymus praecox arcticus coccineus*	N	Summer
Red Maids *Calandrinia ciliata*	N & P	Spring-Summer
Rocky Mountain Bee Plant *Cleome serrulata*	N & P	Spring-Summer
Rose *Rosa* spp.	P	Summer-Autumn
Russian Olive *Elaeagnus angustifolia* L.	N & P	Summer
Russian Sage *Perovskia atriplicifolia*	N	Summer-Autumn
Sage *Salvia* spp.	N	Summer
Sagebrush *Artemisia* spp.	P	Summer-Autumn
Sainfoin *Onobrychis viciifolia*	N	Summer
St. John's Wort *Hypericum perforatum* L. (Also Klamath Weed, Tipton Weed and Goat Weed)	N & P	Summer
Salal *Gaultheria shallon*	N	Spring-Summer
Salmonberry *Rubus spectabilis*	N & P	Spring-Summer
Sassafras *Sassafras officinale*	N & P	Spring
Saw Palmetto *Serenoa repens* (Bartr.)	N	Spring

(Major) Scrophularia *Scrophularia* spp. (Also Figwort)	N	Summer
Seagrape *Coccoloba uvifera*	N	Spring-Summer
Self-Heal *Prunella vulgaris*	N	Summer
Service Berry *Amelanchier* spp.	P	Spring-Summer
Skunk Bush *Rhus trilobata*	N & P	Spring-Summer
Skunk Cabbage *Lysichitum americanum* (Not same as Eastern Skunk Cabbage)	P	Spring-Summer
Shadbush *Amelanchier arborea* (Also Juneberry, Servicetree)	N	Spring
Silver Thyme *Teucrium chamaedrys*	N	Summer
Sneezeweed *Helenium autumnale* L. (Also Bitter sneezeweed)	N & P	Summer-Autumn
Snowberry *Symphoricarpos* spp.	N	Spring-Summer
Spearmint *Mentha spicata* L.	N	Summer
Sorghum *Sorghum vulgare*	P	Summer
Soybean *Glycine soja* (Erratic nectar producer)	N	Summer-Autumn
Spanish Needles *Bidens* spp.	N & P	Summer
Spiraea	P	Spring-Summer

Spiraea spp. Speedwell *Veronica spicata*	N	Summer
Spring Vetch *Vicia sativa* L.	N & P	Summer
Spruce *Picea* spp.	HD	Spring-Summer
Sourwood *Oxydendrum arboreum*	N & P	Spring-Summer
Strawberry *Fragaria* spp. (Marginal nectar and pollen plant)	N & P	Spring-Summer
Sumac *Rhus glabra* (Occasionally good crops)	N & P	Summer
Summer Farewell *Dalea pinnata*	N	Autumn
Sunflower (Common) *Helianthus annuus* L. (Good pollen but rarely surplus honey)	N & P	Summer-Autumn
Sweet Corn *Zea mays* (Sometimes field corn)	P	Summer
Sweet Geranium *Geranium pratense* L.	N	Spring-Summer
Sycamore *Platanus occidentalis*	P	Spring
Tall Ironweed *Vernonia altissima*	N	Summer-Autumn
Tansey Ragwort *Senecio jacobaea* L. (Reported to produce honey toxic to humans but not to bees)	N & P	Summer-Autumn
Teasel	N & P	Summer

Dipsacus sylvestris Thistle *Centaurea* spp.	N & P	Summer-Autumn
Thyme *Thymus pulegioides*	N	Summer
Tinker's Penny *Hypericum anagalloides* (Also Water St. John's-wort, Bog St. John's-wort)	N & P	Summer
TiTi *Cliftonia* spp. (See Buckwheat tree, *C. racemiflora* causes Purple Brood)	N & P	Spring
Tree-of-Heaven *Ailanthus altissima*	N & P	Summer
Trefoil *Lotus* spp.	N & P	Spring-Summer
Tupelo *Nyssa* spp. (Also White Tupelo) (Major)	N & P	Spring
Vervain *Verbena* spp. (Also Verbena)	N & P	Spring-Summer- Autumn
Virginia Creeper *Parthenocissus quinquefolia*	N & P	Summer
Vitex *Vitex negundo* L.	N	Summer
Walnut *Juglans* spp.	P	Spring
Watermelon *Citrullus lanatus*	N & P	Summer
Wheat *Triticum* L. (Sap from cut stubble, does not normally result in stored crop)	Sap	Spring-Summer
White Sweet Clover *Melilotus alba*	N & P	Spring-Summer

(Major) White Ash *Fraxinus americana* L.	P	Spring
White Dutch Clover *Trifolium repens* (Good honey plant) (Major)	N & P	Summer
Wild Cherry *Prunus serotina Ehrh.* (Occasional honey crop)	N & P	Spring
Wild Carrot *Daucus carota* (Also Queen Anne's Lace, Bird's Nest Plant, Devil's Plague, Lace Flower)	N	Summer-Autumn
Willow *Salix* spp. (Major pollen producer) (Major)	N & P	Winter-Spring
Wisteria *Wisteria* spp.	N	Spring
Wollypod *Vicia dasycarpa*	N & P	Spring-Summer Autumn
Woodsage *Teucrium canadense* (Also American Germander)	N & P	Summer
Yellow Wood *Cladastris lutea*	N	Spring-Summer
Yellow Poplar *Liriodendron tulipifera* (Also Tulip Poplar, Tulip Tree) (Major)	N & P	Spring-Summer
Yellow Sweet Clover *Melilotus officinalis*	N & P	Spring-Summer
Yerba Santa *Eriodictyon californicum*	N & P	Summer

Appendix 2

BEESWAX CHARACTERISTICS AND USES

Technical Characteristics[22]
1. Melting Point: 147° F, 63° C
2. Solidification Point: 146.3° F
3. Specific Gravity @ 60° F, 15° C: 0.959 – 0.975 (Water=1.00)
4. General Composition: 70–72% esters, 14–15% free ceric acids, 12% hydrocarbons, 1% free alcohols, 1% water and minerals, 0.8% other minor components
5. Saponification Value: 95.34
6. Acid Value: 17.5
7. Solubility:
   A. Insoluble: Water
   B. Slightly soluble: Cold Alcohol
   C. Completely soluble: Fixed or Volatile oils, Benzene, Ether, Chloroform

Production Calculations (Estimations):
1. 6.7–8.8 pounds of honey will produce 1 pound of beeswax
2. 1 pound of beeswax will build 35,000 wax cells
3. 1 pound of beeswax will store 22 pounds of honey
4. A wax scale is approximately 1/8" in diameter and about 1/250" thick
5. 500,000 wax scales per pound
6. Under good conditions, 10,000 bees could produce 1 pound of beeswax in three days.

Processing Precautions:
1. Never use an open flame. Use a double boiler mechanism. Beeswax is highly flammable.
2. Wax will be discolored if heated over 185° F.
3. Using steam to melt wax will damage the wax permanently.
4. Use only Aluminum, Nickel, Tin, or Stainless Steel vessels to process wax. Other metals will discolor beeswax. Smooth pans with tapered sides work best.
5. Propolis should be separated from wax. It lowers the quality of beeswax. Consequently, hive scrapings should not be mixed with high quality cappings wax.
6. Do not store any chemicals or pesticides near beeswax. It readily absorbs residue from such materials.

---

[22]Brown, Ron. 1981. *Beeswax*, Bee Books New and Old. Tapping Wall Farm, Burrowbridge, Summerset, Great Britain.

Uses for Beeswax:

Major Uses:
1. Cosmetics
2. Candles
3. Beeswax foundation
4. Pharmaceuticals
5. Dentistry
6. Foundries
7. Polishes

Minor Uses:
1. Adhesives
2. Crayons
3. Chewing Gum
4. Various waxes (Grafting Wax, Ski Wax, Ironing Wax, Archers' Wax)
5. Various Woodworking Procedures
6. Arts and Crafts Uses

Appendix 3

TREATMENT SCHEDULE

Generalized Treatment Schedule for Honey Bee Diseases and Pests

For Honey Producing Colonies in Temperate Climates

Season	Indicator	Treat For	Comments
Late Winter	1st Pollen Source	Varroa, AFB, EFB, Tracheal, Nosema	• No supers on Nosema treatment secondary to Fall treatment
Spring	Fruit Bloom, Spring Flowers	Varroa, AFB, EFB, Tracheal	• No supers on
Late Spring/ Early Summer	Clovers, Spring Flowers	Tracheal	• Supers on Tracheal treatment with vegetable shortening year round
Summer	Clovers	None	• Supers on
Late Summer /Early Fall	Goldenrod, Asters	AFB, Tracheal, Varroa	• No supers on
Fall	Asters	Nosema, AFB, Varroa, Tracheal	• No supers on
Winter	None	None	

Bibliography and Advanced Readings

1. **Campion, Alan.** *Bees At The Bottom Of The Garden.* London/England: Adam & Charles Black; 1984; ISBN: 0-7136-2433-7.

2. **Caron, Dewey M.** *Honey Bee Biology and Beekeeping.* Cheshire//CT: Wicwas Press; 1999; ISBN: 1-878075-09-8.

3. **Crane, Eva.** *Honey, A Comprehensive Survey.* London/England: Heinemann; 1975; ISBN: 434 90270 5.

4. **Graham, Joe.** *The Hive and the Honey Bee.* Hamilton/IL: Dadant & Sons; 1992; ISBN: 0-915698-09-9.

5. **Hepburn, H. R.** *Honey Bees and Wax—An Experimental Natural History.* New York/NY: Springer-Verlag; 1986; ISBN: 3-540-16918-0.

6. **Hooper, Ted and Taylor, Mike.** *The Beekeeper's Garden.* London/England: Alphabooks Ltd; 1988; ISBN: 0-7136-3023-X.

7. **Kelley, Walter T.** *How to Keep Bees and Sell Honey.* Clarkson/KY: The Walter T. Kelley Company; 1955.

8. **Laidlaw, Harry H. Jr. and Page, Robert E. Jr.** *Queen Rearing and Bee Breeding.* Cheshire//CT: Wicwas Press; 1997; ISBN: 1-878075-08-X.

9. **McGregor, S. E.** *Insect Pollination of Crops.* Washington, D.C.: ARS, USDA; 1976 Jul.

10. **Morse, Roger A. and Flottum, Kim.** *Honey Bee Pests, Predators and Diseases.* Medina, OH: The A.I. Root Company; 1997; ISBN: 0-936028-10-6.

11. **Ribbands, C. R.** *The Behavior and Social Life of Honey Bees.* New York/NY: Dover Publications, Inc.; 1953.

12. **Sammataro, Diana and Avitabile, Alphonse.** *The Beekeeper's Handbook.* Ithaca//NY: Cornell University Press; 1998; ISBN: 0-8014-8503-7.

13. **Snodgrass, R. E.** *Anatomy of the Honey Bee.* Ithaca/NY: Comstock Publishing Associates; 1956; ISBN: 0-8014-0400-2.

14. **Winston, Mark.** *The Biology of the Honey Bee.* Cambridge/MA: Harvard University Press; 1987; ISBN: 0-674-07408-4.

15. **USDA National Agriculture Library Beekeeping resource page:** *http://www2.oardc.ohio-state.edu/agnic/bee/default.htm*

Glossary

A.I. Root - Owner of the first company to manufacture bee hive equipment in the US in Medina, Ohio.

Absconding - The complete abandonment of a hive frequently caused by starvation or by pests.

Acarine disease - Caused by tracheal mite infestations *(see Tracheal mite)*

Acarology - The study of mites.

Africanized honey bees - The notorious "Killer Bee" that was introduced into South America to improve honey bee genetics there. (*Apis mellifera scutellata*).

Afterswarms - Small swarms that leave shortly after the first main swarm and are usually headed by a virgin queen. Also called secondary swarms.

Alarm pheromone - A pheromone produced by worker bees to incite other bees to colony defense. (*Isopentyl acetate*).

American foulbrood (AFB) - A bacterial infection of honey bee larvae caused by *Paenibacillus larvae* (previously called *Bacillus larvae*). Spores cause long-term contamination of equipment.

Apiarist - One who keeps bees

Apiary - A bee yard location.

Apiculture - The science and craft of keeping bees.

Apistan strips - Plastic strips embedded with fluvalinate and used to suppress Varroa mite infestations.

Apitherapy - Procedures using various hive products for therapeutic purposes for humans.

Balling - Balling the queen is the behavior a group of bees surrounding a foreign queen and suffocating or overheating the queen to the point that she dies.

Banking queens - The beekeeper management technique of holding multiple caged queens for later use in other colonies.

Bee blower - A device that generates low pressure, high volume air for blowing bees from supers.

Bee bread - A mixture of pollen and honey prepared by house bees and used to feed developing brood.

Bee escapes - Any of several styles of devices that direct bees in a one-way fashion as in removing bees from supers or from a dwelling.

Bee Go™ - A commercial bee repellent used to drive bees from supers. Normally butyric anhydride.

Bee gum - A section of a hollow tree, used in years past to house a colony of bees.

Bee line - The straight line that bees will follow when returning from a foraging trip or when moving to a new home site.

Bee louse - A flightless ectoparasite of honey bees of minimal importance. Larval forms tunnel beneath honey cappings leaving thread-like damage. (*Braula coeca*)

Bee Parasitic Mite Syndrome - Bee Parasitic Mite Syndrome (BPMS) is apparently a viral secondary infection found in some colonies having Varroa mite infestations.

Bee space - The basic tenet of modern beekeeping hive equipment. Less than 1/4" bees fill with propolis, 1/4"–3/8" bees leave open, greater than 3/8" bees fill with comb.

Bee suit - Protective clothing, including facial protection, worn by beekeepers when working bee hives.

Bee tree - A hollow tree housing a colony of bees. If cut, then called a bee gum. *See Bee gum.*

Beeswax - The basic building material of the bee hive being used for brood production and foodstuff storage. *See Wax glands.*

Box hives - Old-styled hives that were tall boxes with nothing more than a cross brace in the center. This hive did not have removable frames.

Breeder queens - Selected queens used to produce daughter queens for sale.

Brood - All stages of developing bees—egg, larvae, pupa—and is found in the brood chamber.

Brood chamber - The area of the hive where young bees are produced. Usually near the bottom of the hive.

Brood rearing - The process of producing adult bees from egg to adult.

Bulk comb - Honey produced and sold within the original frame.

Burr comb - Also called brace comb and is used to bridge combs within the hive and on tops of frames.

Capped brood - The pupal stage of bee development and sealed with a mixture of wax and propolis.

Cappings - Thin, white new beeswax used to cover new honey.

Cappings scratcher - A device made of thin wire prongs used to puncture capping in preparation for extracting.

Caste system - Two types of female bees within the hive: queen, workers.

Cell - Single components of a comb. Can be either worker, queen, or drone cells. Generally worker and drone cells are also used for storing pollen and nectar.

Cell bar - A slat used to suspend queen cells during the process of queen production.

Cellar wintering - Confining colonies in an unheated cellar during winter months. Not done too much any more and only practical in cold climates.

Chalkbrood - A fungal disease of bee larvae caused by *Ascosphaera apis*. Larvae appear to be white, hard mummies.

Chilled brood - Brood that has dropped below the required incubation temperature and has died.

Chunk honey - A type of honey packaging in which a piece of honey is put into a jar with remaining space filled with liquid honey. Popular in the Southeastern US.

Cleansing flight - A flight during which the rectal contents are evacuated away from the hive.

Cluster - A compact, heat-producing wintering mass of bees.

Colony - The total parts of the nest and its individuals that are housed in a hive.

Comb - The basic component of the colony made from beeswax.

Comb honey - Honey produced and sold within special containers such as basswood boxes or plastic circles. This product is never extracted.

Comb midrib - The center of the comb normally made up of a sheet of foundation.

Compound eyes - The two large eyes on either side of the bee's head and made up of individual facets.

Conical escapes - *See Bee escapes*

Creamed honey - Also called candied honey or spun honey. A controlled granulation process that results in a smooth, butter-like food topping.

Cross-comb - Naturally built comb that is nearly impossible to remove from the colony. Such comb is intertwined and not in straight combs. Colonies are said to be "cross-combed."

Crystallized honey - Honey in which the excess sugar has become solid (precipitated). Heating drives the honey back into solution.

Cut-comb honey - A honey product consisting of a piece of comb honey cut from the frame and sold in a plastic container. This product is never extracted.

Dance language - A recruitment behavior in which successful foragers or scouts re-enact, on the comb surface, a trip to a food source or new home site.

Dearth - A seasonal period of time when there is no nectar, no pollen, or both available for bee foraging.

Deep super - The largest storage available to beekeepers for honey storage. Commonly 9 1/2" deep and routinely used for brood chambers.

Dequeen - A management procedure of removing the reigning queen and replacing her.

Diastase - A honey enzyme.

Dividing colonies - The process of taking part of an established hive, giving it a new queen, and developing another colony from the parent colony. *See Making increase.*

Division board - A piece of equipment used to compartmentalize a hive. May also be called a follower board or a dummy board.

Division board feeder - An internal feeder approximating the size of a deep frame and filled with sugar syrup for bee consumption.

Division of labor - The entire process of addressing all the colony's needs in an organized way with each bee contributing part of the work to complete all the required tasks.

Drawn comb - A completed comb as opposed to foundation.

Drifting - The tendency for returning bees to enter the wrong hive within the yard.

Drip board - A rimmed board, roughly the size of an inner cover that catches honey dripping from removed supers. It is raised off the floor high enough to get a hand truck underneath.

Drone - The haploid male bee.

Drone comb or foundation - Foundation or comb having about four cells per linear inch whereas worker cells have about five cells per linear inch.

Drone congregation areas (DCA) - Apparently arbitrarily selected areas in which drones gather awaiting the nuptial flights of a queen. Assures genetic diversity.

Drone layer - A defective queen producing only drones as her offspring.

Drumming - An old procedure for driving bees up and out of the hive in order to replace the hive equipment. Not done much anymore.

Dwindling - The process of a slow population decline caused by weather conditions or by various hive diseases. *See Spring dwindling.*

Dysentery - A gastrointestinal malady of bees forcing them to defecate within or near the hive. Usually during cold months.

Egg - Normally produced by queens. The first phase of honey bee development that lasts for about three days.

Emergency queen cells - Queens produced from modified worker cells in order to replace a queen that has been abruptly removed for whatever reason.

Emerging brood - Combs containing new adult bees that are chewing their way through cell cappings.

Entrance reducer - Various devices used to restrict the hive entrance to a small opening. Commonly used during winter months or during periods of robbing. Also used to keep mice out of the colony during cool months.

Equalizing brood - Moving brood from a strong colony to a weaker one in order to have all colonies of similar strength.

Escape board - *See Bee escapes*

European foulbrood (EFB) - A bacterial infection of honey bee larvae caused by a bacterium, *Melissococcus pluton* and other bacteria as well. Not generally as serious as AFB.

Extender patty - A mixture of vegetable shortening, sugar, and Terramycin® used to control tracheal mites and to suppress American foulbrood (antibiotic extender patty). *See Grease patty.*

Extracted honey - A type of honey that is uncapped and, using centrifugal force, is spun from the combs. This honey is sold as a liquid with no comb.

Extractor - A barrel-shaped piece of equipment used to sling honey from the combs.

Eyelets - Brass or aluminum cylinders used to reinforce the holes in end bars through which the support wire passes. Otherwise the taunt wire would cut into the end bars.

False queen - An advanced stage of laying worker. This bee actually resembles a queen and conducts herself as a queen but can only produce drones.

Fanning - Frequently at the entrance, bees will fan their wings vigorously to cool the hive or to direct other bees to the hive entrance.

Feces - Honey bee waste products usually voided outside the colony.

Feeder - Any of several styles of devices used to provide sugar syrup or dry sugar to the bee colony.

Feeder shell - An empty super that protects a feeder can on the top of a hive. The can may be on the frames or over the handhold within the inner cover. *See Feeder.*

Feral bees - "Wild" bees that are not managed by a beekeeper. *See Bee tree.*

Fermentation - The degradation of honey through the action of various yeasts. Honey with moisture higher than 18.6% water is prone to fermentation and will turn to a vinegary sour product.

Fertile queen - A queen that has mated with drones and is capable of producing both fertilized and unfertilized eggs.

Festoon (Festooning) - A cluster of bees, formed by individual bees grasping each other to form a lattice-work of bees. This pliable formation is affected by gravity and is used to build combs perpendicular with the ground.

Field bees - Forager bees.

Flight path - The most common and unobstructed direction of flight from the colony entrance.

Forager bee - An individual bee out gathering either: water, pollen, nectar, propolis, or water.

Foundation - An embossed beeswax sheet used by the bees as a template for comb construction.

Frame - Usually made of wood, fitted with foundation, and is used to support beeswax comb. May also be made of plastic.

Frame spacers - Slotted devices that fit into the rabbets of the super and space the frames an equal distance apart with little effort from the beekeeper.

Fumidil-B® - Fumagillin compound used to control Nosema disease.

Fume board - An absorbent-coated board the size of an inner cover. Various chemical bee repellents are poured onto the absorbent pad and is used to drive bees from supers.

Grafting - The process of transferring larva to queen cups for subsequent queen cell development. In reality, not a true graft.

Grease patty - A small cake made of vegetable shortening and sugar and used to control Tracheal mites. *See Extender patty also.*

Green honey - *See Unripe honey.*

Grooming - The process of one bee cleaning another.

Heptanone (2-heptanone) - An alarm pheromone produced by the mandibular glands of worker bees.

Hive - The colony's physical home.

Hive odor - The unique smell that each colony has. Individual guard bees use hive odor to determine if a returning bee should be admitted or not.

Hive scale - Any device used for weighing bee colonies in order to make management decisions.

Hive stand - Any of several designed structures used to support the hive off the ground.

Hive tool - Commonly called a window-opener in the construction trade. Used to pry hive appliances apart and to scrape propolis and wax when necessary.

Homeostasis - Principle describing all things being in balance as determined by biological feedback mechanisms.

Honey - The food produced by the enzymatic inversion of long chain sugars in nectar and the evaporation of water to less that 18.6%. An excellent carbohydrate source.

Honeydew - The sweet, sticky byproduct produced by an aphid infestation. Occasionally produced in quantities great enough to produce a low-quality honey crop for bees.

Honey flow - *See Nectar flow.*

Honey house - The facility used for processing honey and wax.

Honey stomach - An elastic internal bulb used for forage bees to transport nectar. Also called the crop.

Hopelessly queenless - A colony that has no queen nor brood of appropriate age from which to produce a new queen.

House bee - The stage of an adult bee's life when she works building combs and cleaning the hive.

Hybrid queens - Specific breeds of queens derived by crossing selected lines in order to develop desirable characteristics.

Hygroscopic - The general ability of anything to absorb water from the air. Honey is hygroscopic.

Hypopharyngeal glands - The brood food glands of nurse bees.

Instrumental insemination - The mechanical fertilization of honey bee queens using specialized equipment and semen from known sources. Used to produce hybrid queens. Frequently called artificial insemination.

Invertase - An enzyme used by bees to invert complex sugars into simple ones. Critical in honey processing.

Isle of Wight Disease - *See Tracheal mites or Acarine disease*

Isopentyl acetate - Alarm pheromone produced by the sting gland.

Italian bee - *Apis mellifera ligustica.* The most common honey bee race in the US.

Kelley, Walter T. - Beekeeper and founder of the *Walter T. Kelley Bee Supply Company* in Clarkson, KY.

Langstroth hive - The early hive design, used today in simplified form, that was developed by L.L. Langstroth, a Presbyterian minister from Pennsylvania.

Larva - The grub or worm stage of honey bee metamorphosis. The second stage (egg, larva, pupa, adult)

Laying worker - Workers that have not been hormonally suppressed by pheromone secretions from a fertile queen. Only drones are produced by laying workers. *See False queen.*

Line queens - Queens that are untested and sold directly to beekeepers.

Making increase - To increase colony numbers by any given process. *See Dividing colonies.*

Mandibles - Insect jaws. Used by honey bees to build comb and to grasp hive litter or enemies.

Marked queen - A queen having had a distinctive mark, usually enamel paint, put on her thorax by the beekeeper. Used for either finding the queen or for telling her age.

Mating flights - Only taken during the early stages of her life, nuptial flights taken by a young queen when she mates. She never mates again.

Mating sign - Part of the male genetalia that remains attached to the queen after she mates. Worker bees remove it.

Mead - A honey wine made from controlled honey fermentation.

Menthol crystals - Crystals from the mint family *Mentha arvensis.* Used to control tracheal mites. *See Tracheal mites or Acarine disease.*

Metamorphosis - System of physiological development by passing through specific stages. Honey bees undergo complete metamorphosis having the stages of: egg, larva, pupa, and adult.

Migratory beekeeping - Beekeepers who move their colonies from site to site for either honey production, pollination or both.

Moveable frame - A colony having suspended frames that can be removed for inspection or for management reasons. Such frames are required by regulation in most US states.

Nasonov glands - A scent gland used by bees to help other bees find their way to the hive, to water, or to a nectar source.

Native bees - Local species of bees other than honey bees. Bumble bees and leaf cutter bees are examples of native bees. Sometimes called wild bees.

Nectar - A sugar-solution reward, produced by plant nectaries, and offered by some plants to pollinators. Honey bees use nectar to produce honey. *See Nectar flow.*

Nectar flow - Seasonal period when plants are producing nectar that bees can convert to honey. Sometime called a honey flow.

Nectar guides - Coloration on blossoms that direct foragers to the nectar source within the blossom. Frequently ultraviolet colored, therefore invisible to humans.

Nosema apis - See Nosema and Fumidil-B™ (fumagillin)

Nosema Disease - A protozoan (*Nosema apis*) that attacks the digestive track of honey bees, causing dysentery and premature death of individual bees. Controlled by fumagillin. *See Fumidil-B.*

Nucleus hive - Generally just a small hive having either fewer frames than a full-sized hive or having smaller frames than common frames. Sometimes called a "nuc."

Nurse bees - Individual bees at a stage in their lives where they are responsible for feeding young bees.

Observation hive - A hive having either glass or Plexiglas panels for viewing the internal workings of a bee colony. Many styles exist.

Osmophilic yeasts - Yeasts responsible for honey fermentation.

Out apiary - An outyard or an apiary site away from the home apiary.

Outyard - *See Out apiary.*

Outer cover - The outer top of the bee colony. The inner cover is underneath the outer cover. Can be either a telescoping outer cover or a single piece migratory outer cover.

Ovary - Egg-producing organs. In honey bees, primarily found in the queen and are vestigial in workers.

Oxytetracycline - Terramycin™. Antibiotic used to suppress American foulbrood.

Package bees - Caged bees purchased to make colony number increase. Commonly, three pounds per cage and containing a new, separately-caged queen.

Paradichlorobenzene (PDB) - Fumigant chemical used to control wax moths. A similar fumigant, naphthalene, should not be used.

Paralysis, honey bee - Apparently a viral malady of adult honey bees. Bee are unable to fly or work and crawl in front of the colony. No control measures exist for this disease, but it appears to be self-limiting.

Pheromones - Chemical secretions that instinctively direct bees to perform various functions or behaviors. Used by bees extensively.

Piping - A combat sound made by young queens as they search each other out for mortal combat. Queens still confined to queen cells are said to "quack" or "toot" in response to released queens' piping.

Plant fidelity - The tendency of foraging bees to work a single plant species. Appropriate pollen transfer is achieved in this way.

Play flights - Orientation flights taken by young worker bees as they learn their environment.

Plumose hairs - The branched hairs that completely cover a bee's body. Useful in accumulating pollen.

Polariscope - A simple device using polarized light to look through bottled honey for contaminants such as lint or bee parts. Used by honey judges.

Pollen - The male portion of a blossom required by a specific plant to produce seeds and fruit. Required by bees as a protein source.

Pollen basket - A basket formed by honey bee hairs on the rear-most legs and is used to transport pollen back to the nest.

Pollen insert - A device containing viable pollen and placed at the entrance of a colony. Foragers must walk through the pollen on their way to blossoms, which they then transport to compatible blossoms. Pollination of specific crops is reported to be increased.

Pollen patty - A pollen supplement made of pollen and other protein-rich foods. Use to build up colony populations in the spring. Also pollen supplement. *See Pollen substitute.*

Pollen substitute - A protein-rich food intended to completely replace pollen within the colony. Used to build up colony population. *See Pollen patty.*

Pollen trap - A device that scrapes the pollen loads from returning foragers and collects it in a storage container. Many styles are available.

Pollination - Fertilization caused by appropriate pollen being deposited on the pistil of the blossom. Plants use many diverse pollinating agents to transfer pollen.

Prepupa - The brief stage between the larval and pupa forms. Essentially the coiled larvae stretch out lengthwise before beginning the transition to pupae.

Prime swarm - Normally the first swarm to issue from a colony during a given season. Also called a primary swarm. *See Afterswarms.*

Proboscis - The soda-straw-like structure used for collecting nectar and water by field bees.

Propolis - Bee glue or bee caulking. Made of resins collected from trees and buds and used to seal the colony and as a component in brood cappings. Thought to have antibiotic characteristics.

Pupa - In complete metamorphosis, the third stage of development. Egg, larva, pupa, and adult.

Queen - The chemical and genetic leader of a colony. The queen is a diploid female that produces all the brood within the colony and is responsible for specific pheromone production.

Queen cage - A cage used to contain a queen for shipping or introduction. Many designs exist.

Queen cell cup - A queen cell that is not in use. A cup becomes a cell once an egg is placed in it. A cup can be used several times if necessary.

Queen cells - Peanut-shaped cells used to incubate new queens. Three types are: emergency, supersedure, and swarm cells.

Queen excluder - A grid with spacing large enough for worker bees to pass but restrictive to both queens and drones. Used to keep brood out of the honey supers.

Queenright - A colony having an established queen

Queen substance - A pheromone produced by the queen that inhibits the production of new queens. (9-oxo-2-decenoic acid) Also called 9 ODA.

Queen tab - A small piece of an Apistan™ strip. Used to suppress Varroa within the queen cage during shipping.

Rabbet - In woodworking, a groove running with the grain and used in beekeeping equipment to form the ledge on which frames are suspended. Normally 5/8" deep and cut into the hive body ends along the top edge.

Races of bees - Honey bees adapted to specific conditions and environments. The Italian honey bee is a common honey bee race.

Refractometer - A hand-held device for measuring the water content of honey.

Rendering wax - Melting wax cappings and comb residue into wax cakes.

Requeening - The process of replacing a queen within a specific colony.

Reversing - The management process of exchanging positions of brood chambers and later in the season changing the position of supers.

Robbing - The behavior of foragers from one colony taking stores from another, usually weaker, colony. Normally happens when no nectar is available in the field. Whenever possible, robbing should be avoided by the beekeeper. Possible way for disease spread.

Robbing screen - A device that allows departing bees to leave, but confuses robber bees when they attempt to enter. Only useful for a few days.

Round dance - Dance performed when the food source is within ten meters of the hive.

Round sections - Comb honey appliances used to produce circular pieces of comb honey. Frequently called Ross Rounds®.

Royal jelly - A food rich in hormones and protein, fed by nurse bees to developing queens throughout their development. Worker bees are only fed royal jelly for the first few days of their lives. *See Worker jelly.*

Sacbrood - A viral disease of honey bee brood. No current control exists, but the disease is normally not a serious problem.

Scout bee - An individual bee searching for a new nest cavity or for food and water resources.

Section honey - Comb honey produced in special basswood boxes.

Settling tank - Usually a stainless steel tank in which honey is allowed to sit for a few days in order for extraneous materials to float to the top. Air bubbles, wax, and bee body parts are examples of things that would settle out.

Shallow super - Normally a super having a depth of about 4-1/2".

Shotgun brood pattern - A spotty pattern caused by a poor queen or by disease.

Skep - A beehive domicile made from woven straw in a dome-shape form. Used in the US only as an antique or as an ornament. Frames were not removable in most skeps. European in origin.

Slumgum - The dark, wax residue remaining after wax has been rendered.

Small Hive Beetle - The Small Hive Beetle (SHB) *Aethina tumida* is a small, nearly square, reddish-brown beetle whose adults and larvae attack honey bee hives and stored honey in combs.

Smoker - A beekeeper appliance used to suppress the defensive behavior of guard bees. It is useful in reducing the stinging response of bees.

Solar wax melter - A box with a glass lid that uses solar energy to melt wax. Though cheap, it is not very efficient.

Spermathaeca - Structure within the queen used to store sperm.

Spiracles - Openings to the bee's respiratory system.

Split or splits - Making colony increase by dividing other colonies. *See Dividing colonies or Making increase.*

Spring dwindling - Population decline in the spring caused by disease or by limited food stores.

Sting or stinger - The defensive weapon of the honey bee.

Sucrose - A long-chain common sugar best known as table sugar but also present in nectar. House bees reduce this sugar to glucose and fructose as they process it into honey.

Super - Additional space supplied by the beekeeper for the bees to store surplus honey. An old term used to denote something in excess or above the minimum. Supers are manufactured in several different depths.

Supersedure - Natural replacement of a failing queen. Sometimes spelled supercedure.

Supering - The management process of adding supers.

Surplus honey - The part of the honey crop that the beekeeper takes for him/herself while leaving enough for the bee colony to prosper.

Swarm - Colony fission. A colony splits, roughly in half, and the split finds a new nest cavity and begins a second colony. The old queen goes with the swarm.

Swarming season - The time of the year, usually early spring, when bee colonies are most likely to increase numbers. *See Prime swarm.*

Terramycin™ - *See Oxytetracycline.*

Thorax - The center portion of the bee's body and the center of locomotion. The wings and the legs are attached to the thorax.

Top bar - The uppermost part of a frame onto which both end bars are attached and from which the comb is suspended.

Trachea - The breathing tube component of the bee's respiratory system and used to transport air.

Tracheal mite - A small mite that invades the respiratory system of honey bees (*Acarapis woodi*). *See Acarine disease.*

Transitional cells - Comb cells that are neither worker nor drone cells but are in between.

Travel stain - The discoloration that occurs to new, white cappings as bees walk over it, probably caused by pollen and propolis pigmentation.

Trophallaxis - Food exchange between hive members. Not necessarily the same as food sharing. Required to provide each hive member with necessary hive pheromones.

Two-Queen system - A honey production system using two queens to build up population faster. Normally, one queen is removed just before the nectar flow begins.

Uncapped brood - Either the egg or larval stages of bee brood. Also called open brood.

Uncapping knife - Any kind of knife used to cut wax cappings from honey combs. Usually heated in some way. May be highly mechanized.

Unfertilized egg - Is haploid in number and will result in a drone bee. Can be laid either by mated queens or by laying workers.

Uniting - The process of combining colonies usually in preparation for winter months.

Unripe honey (green honey) - Honey that has not yet been reduced to moisture content of less that 18.6% moisture. Such honey is likely to ferment. Occasionally called green honey.

Unsealed brood - *See Uncapped brood.*

Upper screen - Also called division screen for either separating one part of the hive from another or for closing the top of the colony for transporting.

Varroa mite - A large parasitic mite (*Varroa jacobsoni*) that attacks both brood and adult bees. If left untreated, most colonies will die from mite feeding damage.

Venom - Complex chemical produced by glands near the stinger of the honey bee and causes pain when injected into potential enemies of the colony.

Ventriculus - The true stomach of the honey bee and responsible for digestion.

Virgin queen - A young adult queen that has not taken nuptial flights.

Wag-tail dance (Waggle dance) - Dance performed when the food source is within 100 meters of the hive.

Washboarding - A scouring movement, sometimes called rocking, in which bee appears to be cleaning or polishing the landing board. Behavior not understood.

Wax bloom - A crystalline powdery substance that appears on stored wax. It causes no harm and cannot readily be avoided.

Wax glands - Four pairs of abdominal glands located on the bottom surface of the bee's body and used to produce virgin wax to be used within the colony. *See Wax scales.*

Wax moth (Greater) - A Lepidopterous pest of combs. The larvae of *Galleria mellonella* tunnel through comb while searching for protein and carbohydrates. Combs are destroyed.

Wax scales - A single piece of wax, recently produced by the wax glands, before the bee has processed it by chewing and shaping. Wax scales are frequently dropped during times when combs are being built. For some unknown reason, they are not retrieved and will be found on the bottom board.

Wheast - A common yeast component of pollen supplements. Provides protein to the mixture.

Windbreaks - Any thing or device that diverts wind away from bee hives.

Wing hooks - Small hooks on the hind wings used to hook front wing and back wing together before taking flight. Also called hammuli.

Winter cluster - *See Cluster.*

Winter hardy - The ability of some strains of honey bees to withstand winter conditions better than other strains.

Wire embedder - Various devices used to either press or melt foundation wires into foundation sheets. Provides for added comb strength.

Worker bee - The common honey bee that maintains the hive, gathers water and nectar, and pollinates plants. Though diploid, workers are sterile.

Worker jelly - The basic food fed to worker bees during their development. Compare to royal jelly which is the principle food fed to queen bees during development.

Wrapping colonies - The management process of enclosing a hive with a protective covering in preparation for winter. Also called packing. Performed only in cold climates.

Index

abdomen 112
absconding 175
Acarapis woodi 167
Aethina tumida Murray 168
Africanized honey bee 174
afternoon shade 67
afterswarms 43
American foulbrood 160
antenna cleaner 110
antennae 108
ants 170
Apis mellifera L 79
Apistan® 166
avoiding a bee sting 106
battens 69
bee beards 44
bee blower 135
bee bread 153
bee paralysis 164
bee scouts 89
bee space 16
bee suit 32
bee vacuum 196
bee venom 106
beekeeping gardeners 79
beeswax 180
beeswax candles 182
Boardman feeder 62
bottom bar 27
bottom board 19
brace comb 92
brands 23
brood 52
brood chamber 20
brood food 103
bumble bees 77
burr comb 92
butyric anhydride 135
candy boards 64
capped honey 60
caste system 96
cell base 90
cell shapes 90

Check Mite+® 169
chorion 103
clusters 53
color vision 109
comb builder 97
comb fillers 64
combining colonies 52
commercial beekeepers 153
commercial pollination 153
complete metamorphosis 99
compound eyes 109
cone trap 84
corn starch 65
corn syrup 65
coumaphos 169
creamed honey 141
crop 112
cut-comb 139
Dadant, C.P. 194
dance language 94
diploid (female) eggs 103
disease spread 160
division board feeders 62
Doolittle, G.M. 121
drip board 200
drones 98
dry feed 64
dry sugar 65
dry swarms 43
eggs 100
emergency cell 117
end bar 27
entrance 55
entrance reducer 20
esophagus 109
established colonies 35
European foulbrood 162
external feeders 62
eyelets 30
eyes 109
facets 109
false queens 125
feeders 61
fermentation 128
flight muscles 110
fluvalinate 166

foundation 30
friction-top feeders 63
frost 55
frost pockets 67
fructose 128
Fumidil-B® 164
fume boards 135
Galleria mellonella (L.) 171
gardens 77
GardStar® 170
gloves 32
glucose 128
glucose oxidase 128
granulated corn syrup 65
granulation 128
gravity 95
gross weight 54
hair 108
hand trucks 71
haploid 103
head 108
high-fructose corn syrup 65
hive management 46
hive stand 17
hive tool 33
hive top feeders 63
honey sac 112
honey supers 21
house bee 153
hydrogen peroxide 128
hypopharyngeal gland 103
hypopharyngeal glands 109
inner cover 21
instrumental insemination 119
internal feeders 62
invertase 128
junk sugar 65
Langstroth, L. L. 193
larva 102
latex paint 25
laying workers 102
leaf-cutter bees 78
legs 109
mandibles 109
mandibular glands 110
marginal wing hooks 110

mead 190
menthol 168
mice 173
micropyle 104
Miller, C.C. 199
morning sun 67
mouthparts 109
moving colonies 68
must, the 191
Nasonov gland 94
National Honey Board 143
native bees 78
nectar 13
nectar flow 133
neighbors 67
nervous system 112
nosema 47
Nosema apis 163
nucleus hive 79
nucs 123
nurse bees 122
observation hives 186
open feeding 61
Osmia 79
package bees 37
Paenibacillus (Bacillus) larvae 160
pesticide 67
pheromones 93
plastic frames 29
polariscope 130
pollen 13
pollen pellet 153
pollen substitute 156
pollen substitutes 48
pollen trapping 154
pollination contracts 154
Porter Bee Escape 134
prime swarm 43
proboscis 109
progressive robbing 76
propolis 27
prothoracic spiracle 167
pupae 99
purchasing colonies 35
queen 116
queen cage 120

queen cells 117
queen cups 92
queen excluder 20
raccoons 171
ratchet straps 69
record keeping 87
requeen 119
robber cage 75
robbing 74
round dance 94
sacbrood 164
salivary glands 109
scent gland 112
scenting 42
secondary swarms 43
section comb honey 140
section honey 139
skep 81
skunks 18
slatted rack 199
slumgum 182
small hive beetle 168
smoker 32
smoker fuels 33
solar wax melters 181
sperm 118
spermatheca 118
spur wire embedder 30
staples 68
sting 105
sting lancets 112
sting symptoms 105
sugar candy 64
sugar syrup 60
sunlight 56
supersedure 117
supplemental feeding 60
swarms 41
thorax 109
top screens 70
towing strap 73
Tracheal Mites 167
transferring colonies 83
transitional comb 92
transportation screens 70
trap box 197

two-queen system 145
vaginal valvefold 104
Varroa Mites 164
vegetable oil patties 168
veil 31
venom sac 106
ventilation 54
virgin queen 123
Von Frisch, Karl 95
Wagner, Samuel 194
wagtail dance 94
wasps 42
water source 67
wax combs 90
wax glands 112
wax mirrors 180
wax moths 171
wet supers 76
wild nest 89
windbreaks 67
wings 110
winter feed 65
wire embedder 30
worker bees 13
workers 97
yellowjackets 42